Contract Ethics

Studies in Social, Political, and Legal Philosophy

General Editor: James P. Sterba, University of Notre Dame

Contract Ethics:
Evolutionary Biology and the Moral Sentiments

Howard Kahane

ROWMAN & LITTLEFIELD PUBLISHERS, INC.

ROWMAN & LITTLEFIELD PUBLISHERS, INC.

Published in the United States of America
by Rowman & Littlefield Publishers, Inc.
4720 Boston Way, Lanham, Maryland 20706

3 Henrietta Street
London WC2E 8LU, England

British Cataloging in Publication Information Available

Library of Congress Cataloging-in-Publication Data

Kahane, Howard, 1928-
Contract ethics : evolutionary biology and the moral sentiments /
Howard Kahane.
p.   cm.
Includes bibliographical references and index.
1. Ethics.   2. Contracts—Moral and ethical aspects.   3. Ethics,
Evolutinary.   4. Sense (Philosophy)   I. Title.
BJ1031.K23   1995   171'.7—dc20   95-33953   CIP

ISBN 0-8476-8117-3 (cloth: alk. paper)
ISBN 0-8476-8118-1 (pbk.: alk. paper)

Printed in the United States of America

⊗™ The paper used in this publication meets the minimum requirements of
American National Standard for Information Sciences—Permanence of
Paper for Printed Library Materials, ANSI Z39.48–1984.

To my brother, Seymour Kahane, who played the game fair and square, and never, ever, betrayed anyone.

Contents

Preface

There has been a controversy started of late . . . concerning the general foundation of Morals; whether they be derived from Reason, or from sentiment; whether we attain the knowledge of them by chain of argument and induction, or by an immediate feeling and finer internal sense; whether, like all sound judgment of truth and falsehood, they should be the same to every rational intelligent being, or whether, like the perception of beauty and deformity, they be founded entirely on the particular fabric and constitution of the human species.

—David Hume

The essence of virtue is trustworthiness and of vice betrayal.

—Harold Gordon

Although Socrates certainly overstated the case when he said that the unexamined life is not worth living, a certain amount of thought on the matter surely is in order. This is especially true with respect to the moral side of human existence. When, if ever, does it make sense to benefit others at our own expense? When, if ever, are we *obligated* to benefit others at our own expense? Are there overarching moral principles from which the answers to specific moral problems can be deduced? What does morality dictate anyway?

The chief difficulty encountered by anyone looking for answers to these questions is that there is no consensus among the philosophers and theologians who are supposed to be the experts in the field. Over the years, philosophers have provided hundreds of answers for every question. How can even a rather industrious person separate the few grains of philosophical wheat from the malnourishing chaff?

One way is by consulting recently proposed scientific theories concerning the evolution of the human moral repertoire—theories that have been gaining increasing support in recent years. Discovering how we got here may well be the key to understanding where "here" is. Although the details of this evolutionary story are still very much in dispute, there no longer can be much doubt that the sentiments commonly thought of as moral evolved because they enabled our distant ancestors to gain the advantages of cooperative behavior. Human beings are the cooperating animal par excellence, and cooperation requires the trust that moral sentiments are designed to foster. That is why most of us, in one degree or another, are stocked with moral sentiments favoring the making and keeping of fair cooperative and competitive agreements.

But moral sentiments do not always win the day. They must compete with older, self-regarding sentiments that frequently motivate betrayal. Sainthood, in the lingo of the evolutionary biologist, is not an "evolutionarily stable strategy." That is why only fools trust blindly, and why deciding who and when to trust constitutes one of life's more important tasks. It also is one reason why it isn't easy to decide when we ourselves want to be *trustable*.

Well, then, when *do* we want to be trustable? When, if we are rational, *ought* we to want to be trustable? The answer suggested by evolutionary theory is that we want to be trustable when, in certain kinds of circumstances, we have agreed, implicitly or explicitly, to cooperate or compete in a specified manner. *Agreement* is the moral binder, the generator of moral obligation; "Thou shalt keep one's word," the overarching moral precept.

This should make it clear that the theory to be proposed is essentially a contractual one, based on the Hobbesian idea that our (admittedly imperfect) ability to make and keep cooperative agreements is the chief reason why, over the years, life has become less nasty, brutish, and short. It differs from Hobbes's position concerning the sorts of contracts most intelligent human beings would agree to (all-powerful sovereigns having proved to be not a very good idea) and in stressing a feature of moral life to which Hobbes paid insufficient attention, namely the ordinary human desire to keep fair contractual agreements. The question to be investigated, then, is what sorts of bargains a rational person who is *fair minded* would want to strike *and keep* when engaged in the cooperative and competitive activities of everyday life.

Along the way, it will be argued that being faithful in this way is not merely a matter of long-term prudence, as several recent contractualists (e.g., David Gauthier) have claimed. While it is true that prudence alone frequently justifies the keeping of agreements, it doesn't do so in crucial cases. Crime does sometimes pay, and pay very well. When we refrain from breaking agreements in those cases, we do so out of a sense of obligation that overrides the merely prudential considerations tempting us to sin. Moral sentiments counsel loyalty, even at the risk of failure, rather than victory via the betrayal of others. Aristotle was wrong in characterizing human beings as the animal species whose difference is rationality; we are equally differentiated from other animals by our strong desire to keep our word—to play the game fair and square.

It also should be clear from the references to moral sentiments that the theory to be elucidated here is grounded in a subjectivist view of moral obligation. It takes seriously the idea that there are no *objective* moral features of reality and that the fundamental data of ethics are internal sentiments, feelings, desires, and interests. It thus fits nicely with Hume's belief that morality derives not from reason, as Kant and some other objectivists have claimed, but from sentiment; is known not "by chain of argument and induction" but "by an immediate feeling and finer internal sense"; and is founded, "like the perception of beauty and deformity, . . . entirely on the particular fabric and constitution of the human species."

Anyone who takes this tack is confronted with the disagreeable fact that human beings living in the diverse cultures that have existed at one time and place or another have professed adherence to radically different moral codes. This diversity suggests that there are no moral sentiments or moral principles shared by all, or even a large portion, of the human species. (It also suggests that moral standards are cultural in origin, not biologically based, an idea to be discussed shortly.) Underlying this diversity, however, are several ways in which the moral attitudes, dispositions, and belief systems of peoples around the world are a good deal more alike than they are different. Human beings everywhere tend to see the keeping of fair bargains as morally obligatory and, in relatively simple cases, agree as to which sorts of agreements are fair. They find theft and lying odious (although what counts as theft or lying depends on the kinds of agreements, often implicit, the citizens of a given society have struck). But however these practices are conceived, their proscription is universal.

So the moral theory to be elucidated here rests in part on the belief that a modicum of intersubjective agreement concerning the peculiarly moral constraints on behavior can be reached between thinking members of most cultures. The rejection of objective moral systems need not force moral theorists into the abyss of cultural relativism.

Readers who favor an objective approach to moral theory, and therefore reject the subjective philosophical underpinnings of this work, should note that an objective theory of contractual fairness is embedded in it and can be considered apart from the subjective portions of the theory championed here. This does not put the lie to the claim of subjectivity previously stated, but it does bring to the fore the age-old question, "Why be moral?", addressed here as the question "Why keep fair agreements?" The only answer open to an ethical subjectivist is that, on the whole, we ought to keep fair bargains simply because we want to. Morality is self-imposed.

Another philosophical underpinning of this work, dovetailing nicely with the ones just mentioned, is the idea that being a rational, sensible person implies trying to maximize one's desires and attempting to satisfy one's sentiments (over the long run, of course), including those desires and sentiments commonly thought of as moral. Still another is the belief that a great many moralists have lumped together in one jumble, labeled *moral,* several related but nevertheless importantly different sorts of sentiments and desires that need to be separated if we are to make sense of the moral side of life. What is crucial, of course, as John Wisdom and others have been at pains to point out, is not which of these similar items we label with the honorific title *moral,* although we should have reasons for dividing the pie in the way we do. Rather it is that we understand as much as we can about these sentiments, whatever labels we attach to them, and grasp how they affect the decisions made by the rational agents who possess them.

In any case, those inclined towards a very broad conception of moral obligation might note several virtues of the narrower approach taken here. One is that contractual obligations are the hardest to deny. If having promised (in the absence of coercion, trickery, etc.) does not generate a moral obligation, then what does? If we cannot demand that others keep their promises to us, what can we demand from them? At the very least, then, a contractual theory forms an important part of any broader theory of moral obligation.

Another virtue of the contractual approach is that everyday observation and a good deal of recent scientific theory support the idea, mentioned before, that rules requiring the keeping of fair agreements are shared by a large majority of the individuals living at virtually every time and place. Most of the various other moral rules of conduct reflect in one way or another the customs or mores of particular cultures. And still another virtue, related to the first two, is that sentiments favoring the keeping of promises constitute a core standard acceptable to virtually all members of the large, pluralistic societies characteristic of modern life. The chief hope for a peaceful and prosperous future may well depend on our finding ways to replace vicious competitive activities with cooperative practices and principles of the kinds championed here.

My mentor, Hans Reichenbach, believed that philosophical theories about morality should be put forth as *proposals* to be fought over in the political arena, not promulgated as revelations of ultimate, unchangeable, and indubitable truth. It is in this spirit that the theory to be discussed is recommended to you, with the hope that Reichenbach would have found some merit in it.

Most of us have a utopian vision in the back of our minds. Mine is of an ideal world in which everyone is loyal, no one ever betrays or takes advantage of anyone, competition is friendly, and everyone plays the game fairly. It is of a world in which, therefore, "better participants always emerge triumphant." While undoubtedly utopian, this vision does at least dovetail with reality in facing the fact that, along with cooperation, competition is an integral part of human life.

Overview

> [R]eason alone can never produce any action, or give rise to volition. . . . Reason is, and ought only to be, the slave of the passions, and can never pretend to any other office than to serve and obey them.
> —David Hume

The problem in moral philosophy is not that answers to the crucial questions have been scarce but rather that the history of the subject provides those who are interested in moral matters with a plethora of theories concerning moral obligation, fair play, justice, right and wrong, and so on, theories that are incompatible with each other in one way or another. Which, if any, of these theories should we accept?

This work proposes for your consideration and, hopefully, acceptance, a moral theory based on two fundamental principles of fair play that fair-minded individuals can bring to bear when dealing with the problems encountered in everyday life. It is put forth not as received, objective truth about the nature of reality and mankind's place in it, but rather as a theory that, this writer believes, dovetails nicely with deep-seated moral sentiments most of us harbor to one degree or another.

The short first chapter discusses the various ways in which moral introspection, notoriously plagued by self-deception, can be guided by other means, in particular by a consideration of some relatively recent scientific theories that explain the evolution of moral sentiments and the moral side of life. It offers an explanation as to why, in moving from the *is* of moral sentiments to the *ought* of moral obligation, we do not violate David Hume's admonition against reasoning from *is* to *ought*.

Chapter 2 brings to bear some of the recent theories evolutionary biologists have proposed concerning what they call reciprocal and kin altruism, and relates their ideas about reciprocal altruism to the evolution

1

of moral sentiments concerning fair play. Evolutionary forces have in-stilled in us, in varying degrees and patterns, sentiments of fair play in-clining us to enter into and keep the kinds of fair bargains that make for successful cooperative efforts. We play the game straight, when we do, because of these sentiments. We cheat, when we do, because contrary selfish motives also have evolved due to the fact that we all are genetic competitors of each other. The most important fact about the moral side of human nature is that we must cooperate with our most serious ge-netic competitors, so that we frequently are tugged in two different di-rections at once, tempted to sin, yet also motivated to play the game straight. Morality is the oil that lubricates the cooperative social inter-actions which characterize the human repertoire.

Chapter 3 discusses reasons for separating sentiments motivating fair play and the keeping of fair bargains from other sentiments often thought of as moral, for example from those inclining us to be charitable or to sacrifice for close kin.

The first three chapters set the stage. The fourth introduces the two fundamental principles of fair play, one concerning fair competition and the other fair cooperation, that constitute the guts of my proposal. It suggests why, according to evolutionary theory, the vast majority of us are drawn to these standards of fair play in one degree or another, the main reason being that they make possible the many kinds of coopera-tive behavior that are a crucial feature of the human repertoire.

The principle of fair competition to be proposed is the generally ac-cepted one that the rules of a competition are fair only if they are im-partial—only if they do not provide an advantage to one competitor compared to others—so that winners are determined by relevant talents rather than by the rules of the game. The principle of fair cooperation to be championed is the commonly voiced one that the profits (or losses) of a cooperative venture are fairly distributed only if they are divided among the cooperators according to each person's contribution to the common effort.

Sentiments favoring the making and keeping of fair bargains evolved late in the evolutionary game, well after the evolution of those urging us to act selfishly, and also after the evolution of those motivating us to benefit close kin. But they could not have evolved without the con-comitant evolution of sentiments favoring retribution, that is, senti-ments favoring the striking back at those who betray our trust by fail-ing to keep fair agreements, explicit or implicit. The fifth chapter discusses retribution and its cousins, restitution and revenge, and explains why revenge is not a moral concept.

Chapter 6 discusses friendships and degrees of friendliness. It characterizes friendships as based on the advantages of cooperative and reciprocal altruistic behavior, the reason for the evolution of feelings of affection and compassion felt for friends, and of the desire for their welfare. It discusses the difference between friendliness and fairness, and explains why competitive games may be more, or less, friendly, or even very unfriendly, and still be fair.

As stated before, the rules of a competitive game generally are considered to be fair only if they are impartial. But it isn't easy to determine in every case whether a rule is indeed impartial. This problem is discussed in the seventh chapter, where impartiality is characterized in terms of talents relevant to the competitive "games" we wish to play.

Homo sapiens being a (somewhat) rational social animal, group decision procedures are needed to achieve maximal benefits from cooperative activities. Clearly, however, agreements made employing unfair decision procedures are less likely to find favor with those getting the short end of the stick than are bargains arrived at more fairly. Fair group decision procedures are discussed in chapter 8.

The original human in-groups, no doubt, were those of the family and then the clan, or tribe, groups of more or less related individuals. The larger and less genetically cohesive groups that constitute modern societies, states, or nations, evolved from those of the family and clan. Nations and their governments are discussed in chapter 9, along with thoughts about why so-called minimal, or night-watchman, states do not fit the bill as primary human social organizations.

Chapter 10 deals with problems posed by the unfortunate fact that fair play in the social and political arena often conflicts with, and sometimes has to give way to, other considerations. It suggests ways in which these necessary unfairnesses can, at least in part, be rectified in the long run by the enactment of compensating legislation, or by attempts to avoid having the same groups regularly bear the burden when sacrifices for the common good are required.

The theory being proposed here is a subjective one that sees moral obligations as being generated by agreements that are either explicit or implicit. From this point of view, moral rights similarly are generated via agreements of one kind or another. In particular, subjectivists tend to see civil rights as being generated by society-wide agreements (laws) requiring all citizens to relate to others in certain ways. Thus, legislation providing one person with a right, say, to free speech is regarded as generating an obligation in others to refrain from interfering with that liberty. Chapter 11 discusses civil rights, and some related matters.

As remarked earlier, the interests of members of groups of cooperating individuals coincide only in part, given that group members also are competitors. As groups become larger and larger, and less and less genetically cohesive, conflicts of interest increase, and the likelihood increases that legislation will be passed that is unfair to this group (caste, race, religion, gender, economic class) or that. Chapter 12 examines the rational responses open to those unfairly dealt with in this way. It is suggested that rational agents sometimes will have good reason to violate unfair rules and customs, even when these rules have been arrived at by completely fair procedures.

The next three chapters deal with economic fair play. Chapter 13 discusses the vexing issue of capitalistic ("free market") versus socialistic economies. It is argued that either kind of economic system can be fair, or unfair, depending on how it treats one citizen as compared to another. Some of the reasons commonly alleged for believing that capitalistic systems are inherently unfair are discussed, as are similar charges against socialistic economies.

Taxes, like death, being inevitable, at least in any future we or our offsprings' offspring are likely to experience, the question naturally arises as to what sorts of taxes are fair. In chapter 14, fair taxes are characterized primarily in terms of fees for governmental services rendered, an idea that turns out to yield consequences somewhat different than might be supposed on quick reflection. It also is noted that fair tax legislation is possible for purposes of investment in socialistic endeavors, such as the 1930s New Deal Tennessee Valley Authority (TVA) investment in the United States.

As mentioned earlier, considerations of fair play cannot decide the issue between capitalistic and socialistic systems. Indeed, fair-minded citizens might well not select a capitalistic free-market system for their society even if they believed such an economy would produce a greater cornucopia of goods. We do not live by bread, or television sets, alone. Supposing, however, that an electorate does decide to have a capitalistic free-market economy, an immense number of difficult questions concerning fair play and friendly, or unfriendly, competition immediately arise. How friendly a system is the most desirable? (It isn't automatically true that the most friendly system is the best.) How are shares in a cooperative endeavor to be determined when individuals perform such different tasks and some contribute labor or expertise while others provide capital? These and other extremely difficult questions are discussed in chapter 15, where a few guidelines are suggested.

The focus of this work is fairness, and the term *justice* is not mentioned in the first fifteen chapters. Yet others writing on the same or similar topics, John Rawls being perhaps the most prominent example, have used the term *justice* to describe their subject matter. The short sixteenth chapter discusses the relationship between the terms *fairness* and *justice* and suggests that, as often is the case, it doesn't matter which term we use provided we understand what it is we happen to be saying.

One of the important differences between the theory proposed here and most other moral systems is in its concentration on fairness, or justice, to the partial exclusion of other factors often held to be moral. Although, as just noted, it is more important that we understand what is being said rather than which terms are employed, there are several reasons for adopting locutions that separate matters concerning fair play into one group labeled *moral,* with the others placed into another group, here referred to as concerning what it is to be a *good person.* Evolutionary forces have generated in us not just a sense of cooperative and competitive fair play, but also sentiments such as compassion, empathy, and affection that tend to make fair play more likely than it otherwise would be. The label *good person* is reserved here for those who, on the whole, are not only fair-minded but also are well stocked with sentiments of compassion, empathy, and the like, thus being good in the sense, for example, of the biblical Good Samaritan. The concept of a good person is discussed in chapter 17.

The remaining chapters deal with matters related to, but not directly a part of the contractual fair play theory championed in this work. Chapter 18 deals with games, such as prisoner's dilemmas, volunteer's dilemmas, and the like, studied by game theorists, and discusses how these games do in some ways, and do not in others, shed light on the evolution of sentiments favoring cooperative behavior. The issues discussed here have taken on particular importance because of the widespread interest in David Gauthier's writings in which he describes morality as coming into the picture in order to solve problems posed by prisoner's dilemmas.

At the beginning of this overview, it was pointed out that history provides us with an overabundance rather than a paucity of theories about moral right and wrong. Why, then, have so many different sorts of theories found an audience? Chapter 19 tries to explain the appeal of several popular noncontractarian moral theories, such as cultural relativism and utilitarianism. The existence of so many different kinds of moral principles poses a serious problem for ethical subjectivists because it raises the question as to how we can have sentiments favoring (even if just initially, or mistakenly) such a diversity of moral standards.

The next four chapters deal with five contract theories that differ from the one proposed here in one way or another. Chapter 20 deals with John Rawls's theory, perhaps the most widely discussed contract theory proposed in the past hundred years or so. It is argued that where his theory differs from the one championed here, his comes off second best. The great attractiveness of Rawls's theory also is discussed.

Chapter 21 deals with an altogether different sort of contract theory, namely the one proposed by Robert Nozick which generated a good deal of commotion in the 1970s, won Nozick a National Book Award, and seems to have opened the gates to a great many other libertarian moral theories. It is argued that Nozick's ideas are essentially on the wrong track and, in particular, that the minimal state he champions bears little relationship to the societies that human beings have always lived in and, because of our natures, have always preferred.

Chapter 22 deals with the immensely popular theory proposed by David Gauthier that has found great favor, in particular, with many libertarians. Gauthier sees morality as entering the picture when rational agents are confronted with, and solve, problems posed by prisoner's dilemmas, cases where "straightforward" attempts to maximize one's narrow selfish interests fail but "constrained" attempts to do so succeed. It is argued that Gauthier's theory is completely off the mark.

The appearance of Gauthier's work lent fuel to the libertarian fires started by Nozick's book. Chapter 23 discusses, and finds wanting, two more recently proposed libertarian theories that borrow in one way or another from those of Nozick and Gauthier, namely the theories proposed by Tibor Machan and Jan Narveson.

Many theorists reject the kind of meritarian fair-play principle endorsed here in favor of a more egalitarian standard. The attractiveness of egalitarian standards is explained in chapter 24 and the choice of a meritarian standard is defended.

The last chapter, chapter 25, summarizes the theory explained and defended here and ends with a short concluding remark.

A bibliography, listing publications dealing with ethics, evolutionary biology, game theory, and related matters, follows, along with an index.

The Move from *Is* to *Ought*

In every system of morality which I have hitherto met with, I have always remarked that the author proceeds for some time in the ordinary way of reasoning, and establishes the being of God, or makes observations concerning human affairs; when of a sudden I am surprised to find that instead of the usual copulations of propositions, *is,* and *is not,* I meet with no proposition that is not connected with an *ought,* or an *ought not.* This change is imperceptible; but is, however, of the last consequence. For as this *ought* or *ought not,* expresses some new relation or affirmation, it is necessary that it should be observed and explained; and at the same time that a reason should be given for what seems altogether inconceivable, how this new relation can be a deduction from others, which are entirely different from it. But as authors do not commonly use this precaution, I shall presume to recommend it to the readers; and am persuaded, that this small attention would subvert all the vulgar systems of morality, and let us see that the distinction between vice and virtue is not founded merely on the relations of objects, nor is perceived by reason.

— David Hume

Hume's targets in the above quote are those writers who propose allegedly objective moral theories. His underlying claim is that their move from *is* to *ought* cannot be justified. He surely did not mean that there are no facts relevant to moral judgments. On the contrary, he makes it clear elsewhere (for example, in the passage quoted in the Preface to this work) that facts about common human sentiments are indeed relevant. His point is the impossibility of justifying an allegedly *objective* theory of morality by pointing to any kind of *objective* facts.

In any event, there is only one way in which subjectivists can bridge the gap between beliefs or facts about what is the case and those about what ought to be the case, and that is by becoming clear about the immediate feelings and finer internal sense that Hume spoke of. The gap, if there is one for subjectivists, is bridged by discovering the subjective facts about what sorts of obligations we wish to impose on ourselves — and others.

There are various ways in which this can be done, the most obvious, and no doubt the most important, being by means of introspection. But the history of philosophy, if not the history of the human species, shows the difficulty in this line of attack. It isn't that consciences differ from person to person, although that certainly is true, or even that they differ over time in the same person, although that also is true. It is, rather, first, that uninstructed, raw introspection is a notoriously deceptive guide to the deepest human sentiments and desires; and second, that these sentiments and desires tend to contradict one another. The first point should find ready acceptance in this post-Freudian age, given what is now common knowledge about the unconscious mind, rationalization, denial, and so on; the second should be assented to by those who have been tugged forcefully in different directions when wrestling with specific moral problems. This doesn't mean that introspection should be abandoned but simply that what is discovered in this way needs to be evaluated and revised in terms of what can be learned in other ways.

One of these other ways, surely, is by carefully observing what we, and others, *do* when confronted with everyday moral problems. Actions often speak louder than words. Thus, that we are less prepared to sacrifice for remote sufferers than for close friends and compatriots has to count against the idea that very many of us harbor sentiments favoring moral principles requiring us to do so.

While information gleaned from observing ourselves and others in action is without doubt of great value, particularly in seeing through the natural human tendency to hypocrisy, it has the drawback that human beings in daily life sometimes are tempted into doing what they sincerely do not want to do. Actions do not always mirror strongest long-run desires. (Even so, we should note that it is often in the very act of violating deeply felt moral convictions that we are most aware of what those sentiments really are.)

Of course, it goes without saying that the writings of great literary and philosophical figures need to be consulted. The experiences of a single lifetime are rather limited and, in any case, as just remarked, introspective powers frequently are clouded by unconscious forces. The great writers provide us with acute observations on the human condition that it would be rash indeed to pass over.

However, without intending to slight these other sources of correction to immediate introspection, it is to *science* that primary attention will be directed. Some of the recent scientific theories about the evolution of cooperative behavior have a good deal to tell us about human moral sentiments. In the past, philosophers have frequently appealed to the science of their day; doing so now thus follows a long-standing practice. In any event, it would be a mistake to overlook the current scientific theories about the nature of human nature given that they take account of the observations of many investigators and theorizers over several generations.

Unfortunately, there still is a good deal of resistance to the idea that moral behavior has a strong genetic component. Few would deny, of course, that genes play a role; we can't teach cats or cows to behave morally, any more than to speak Swahili. But the fact that moral codes differ so greatly from culture to culture is still often taken to imply that environmental factors, not genes, are the chief determiners of moral sentiments and behavior, and that genes simply move us to accept whatever moral code happens to exist in our own society.

Proponents of this view, however, fail to take account of the fact that the ways in which human beings adapt to a given environment and produce a particular culture are not just random or accidental. They also neglect sociological and other evidence concerning ways in which the moral strictures of all societies are alike.

In any case, surely by now the age-old disputes concerning nature versus nurture have to be seen as wrongheaded. It should be clear by now that biology and culture both play a vital role. So it would be rash to overlook the recent evolutionary biological theories about the nature of human moral behavior and sentiments.

2

Evolutionary Underpinnings

It must not be forgotten that although a high standard of morality gives but a slight or no advantage to each individual man and his children over the other men of the same tribe, yet that an increase in the number of well-endowed men and an advancement in the standard of morality will certainly give an immense advantage to one tribe over another. A tribe that includes many members who, from possessing in a high degree the spirit of patriotism, fidelity, obedience, courage, and sympathy, were always ready to aid one another, and to sacrifice themselves for the common good, would be victorious over most other tribes; and this would be natural selection. At all times throughout the world tribes have supplanted other tribes; and as morality is one important element in their success, the standard of morality and the number of well-endowed men will thus everywhere tend to rise and increase.

—Charles Darwin

Our societies are based on the mammalian plan: the individual strives for personal reproductive success foremost and that of his immediate kin secondarily; further grudging cooperation represents a compromise struck in order to enjoy the benefits of group membership.

—Edward O. Wilson

Civilization is just the jungle by other means.

—Harold Gordon

There once was a time in the history of the earth when moral sentiments and moral behavior did not exist. Now they do. How could this be? Or, to put the question in a more definite form, how did an animal like

Homo sapiens evolve a moral sense and the ability to engage in moral behavior? This is a difficult question to answer, in particular because of the many different ways in which the concept of morality has been conceived of over the centuries. But if we approach the problem by first asking how *unselfish,* or *altruistic,* behavior could have evolved in a world of tooth and claw, answers begin to emerge.

Note first that *genes* are the basic units of natural selection, not species or individual animals and plants. Human beings, as all living things, can profitably be thought of as "gene survival machines" (using the expression introduced by Richard Dawkins).[1] That selfish behavior—behavior likely to increase the survival and reproductive chances of an organism—has genetic survival value seems obvious. In fact, a large majority of the observed behavior of most organisms, including *Homo sapiens,* is of the selfish variety. But there are two kinds of behavior that are in some sense altruistic and yet have genetic survival value, that is, increase the "inclusive genetic fitness" of organisms.

One is *kin altruism,* altruism directed towards close kin. Genes in organisms programmed to engage in certain kinds of kin-altruistic acts clearly have a survival advantage over those in survival machines not so programmed, even though altruistic acts tend to reduce the chances of the survival machines themselves. For example, animals programmed to feed their young tend to reproduce more successfully than competitors not so programmed, notwithstanding the fact that foraging for food takes time and effort and frequently involves risk.

Kin altruism is a very widespread human phenomenon. Offspring in virtually every society receive special care from their parents or other close kin, and sacrifices for relatives are much more common than for other members of the group. Blood *is* thicker than water.

The other fundamental kind of altruism is *reciprocal altruism,* altruism that is directed towards others, kin or nonkin, and that generally is reciprocated. While not as widespread in the animal kingdom as kin altruism, it still is fairly common among higher animals. Examples range from primates grooming and being groomed to the famous cleaner fish who obtain food by cleaning the gills of larger fish in return for not being eaten. This sort of behavior evolves, roughly speaking, because the genetic benefits to each party could not be obtained as easily, or at all, by engaging in other sorts of activities. In the case of primate groom-

---

[1]See his excellent book *The Selfish Gene* (New York and Oxford: Oxford University Press, 1976).

ing, the increase in benefits is obvious, given that individual primates cannot successfully groom themselves and yet grooming is essential for good health.

Grooming illustrates the fine point that reciprocity often is a group practice. Those members of a primate troop who groom others generally will be groomed in turn by other members. But that A grooms B on a given occasion does not mean that B will then groom A in return. Reciprocity for A may come from some other member, who in turn will be groomed by some other member, and so on. (Note that cheaters—those who never groom others, an unusual case—eventually tend to be passed over in the troop grooming ritual.) In human cultures, a great many reciprocal practices are of this group variety: Smith gives directions or aid to Jones but is likely to receive similar benefits from others.

Grooming also illustrates an important kind of reciprocity, namely the *delayed* variety, in which one party provides benefits to another in the expectation of receiving reciprocity at a later time (often from the party originally benefited). Banks, for example, lend money in the expectation of being paid back later (with interest, unfortunately). Delayed reciprocal altruism obviously is riskier than the more immediate variety because the other party has a greater opportunity to "defect" (a technical term), as countless members of human troops do when they fail to pay their bills.

Nevertheless, it is possible and even likely under certain circumstances for delayed reciprocal practices to evolve.[2] They are likely to do so because in the long run and on average they yield a greater genetic payoff than the more selfish kinds of behavior they replace.

But delayed reciprocal altruistic practices have genetic payoffs for the parties who must act first only if their altruistic acts are in fact reciprocated later. So when organisms evolved that were smart enough to keep track, the "strategy" (still another technical term) of only *grudgingly* engaging in reciprocal activities evolved. Indeed, the thrust of a good deal of recent theorizing among evolutionary biologists (e.g., Edward O. Wilson and Richard Dawkins), as well as game theorists (e.g., Robert Axelrod), suggests that human beings should have evolved into

---

[2]A good deal of the recent literature concerning so-called iterated prisoner's dilemmas, to be discussed later, is directed at proving this is true with respect to at least one specialized type. Perhaps the best discussion of the prisoner's dilemma is in Robert Axelrod and W.D. Hamilton, *The Evolution of Cooperation* (New York: Basic Books, 1984).

grudging reciprocators who tend (or at least prefer) to engage in reciprocal activities primarily only with those who prove to be reliable reciprocators in turn. And this is what experience (certainly the experience of this writer) seems to indicate is true of most human beings. We
try very hard to avoid doing business with defectors. Indeed, one of
life's chief tasks is to determine who is reliable, and when, and who not.

The evolution of delayed reciprocal altruistic practices has made possible increasingly sophisticated cooperative activities involving larger and
larger numbers of people. In the modern world, for instance, employees of
large corporations perform their tasks first and only later receive reciprocity in the form of wages; similarly, publishers provide advances to authors
(unfortunately not to this one) in the expectation of one day receiving man-
uscripts whose marketing will prove profitable. Indeed, we can view the
history of the human species in terms of the evolution of cooperative behavior that tends to temper competition among larger and larger groups of
individuals, starting with close kin, moving to nonkin members of larger
and larger in-groups, and then to surrounding out-groups, until in recent
times the benefits of trade have begun to generate what, let us hope, will
develop into friendly worldwide competitive practices replacing the warfare that has so far been a central feature of human existence.[3]

Competition and cooperation thus both are essential ingredients of
the human repertoire. It is this tug in two directions at once — being required to cooperate with other human beings and yet at the same time
to compete with them — that is perhaps the most fundamental fact relevant to the evolution of the moral side of human nature. *Success in life
requires us to cooperate with our most serious genetic competitors!*

The fact that we must cooperate has resulted in the evolution of sentiments likely to increase reciprocal cooperative behavior. That we
must cooperate with genetic competitors has led to the evolution of
countervailing sentiments making cheating (failure to reciprocate)
more probable when it is in our narrow interests than when it is not. It
is being pulled in this way in two directions at once that makes it sensible to speak of the *temptation* to sin, which implies both a desire to
sin and a desire not to. Whether we do or don't in a given situation depends on the relative strengths of these two forces.

---

[3]W. D. Hamilton has an interesting account in chapter 5 of *The Evolution of Cooperation* as to how cooperative practices could and may well have evolved among close kin
and then expanded to include less closely related in-group members.

Of course, we should expect a great deal of variation from person to person, and from time to time, in the relative strengths of these two opposing forces, a theoretical expectation confirmed by even casual observations of human beings in action. No doubt a good deal of this variation is due to environmental differences, but because of the genetic variety found in even the most homogeneous human populations, there also must be a strong genetic cause, just as there is for physical traits such as height. Theory suggests that we should expect saintly types like Mother Teresa to be extremely scarce and sinners like Heinrich Himmler to be somewhat less so, with the rest of us falling somewhere in between, and experience seems to bear this out. (One mark of a well run society, it will be argued later, is the promotion of an environment that tips the scales as much as possible in favor of virtuous behavior.)

If the necessity to cooperate with some of our most serious genetic competitors is the most important fact about human beings relevant to moral theory, the next most important must be that *Homo sapiens* evolved as an in-group/out-group animal. Genetic success (apart from the ongoing battles against fungi, viruses and bacteria) has depended not just on success in competition with members of one's own in-group but on the success of that group in competition with surrounding out-groups. Genetic winners thus have had to play and win two competitive games at once, one with other in-group members, the other with members of competing out-groups.

Before we leave the topic of evolutionary underpinnings, two points need to be stressed. The first is that evolutionary forces have generated not only specific moral sentiments such as those favoring the keeping of fair bargains, but also a more general disposition inclining us to accept and conform to in-group customs and standards — standards that, it needs to be noted, often are in conflict with our more specific moral sentiments.[4] The second point is that in appealing to biological theories, we do not commit the kind of fallacy railed against by David Hume. The claim is not that evolutionary theories can *prove* anything concerning

---

[4]Our brief account in this chapter passes over another point, namely that in the long sweep of human evolution, populations moved to cooperate simply out of prudential considerations would not have fared well against those also motivated by moral tugs of loyalty and a sense of fair play. The point is important because of its relevance to the idea that moral behavior can be justified in terms of very enlightened and prudent self-interest, a claim implicit in the currently very popular writings of David Gauthier (to be dealt with in chapter 22.)

the bindingness of moral obligation but rather that they can, and do, provide very good reasons for believing that most of us should be well stocked with sentiments tending to increase profitable cooperative ventures, sentiments very much of the kind that have generally been thought of as moral. It would be rash indeed to conclude, perhaps upon quick introspection and without taking account of or trying to overcome the various kinds of self-deception that sometimes mislead us as to our true natures, that the cited biological theories are on the wrong track, just as it generally is rash to dismiss theories confirmed by a great many experiences and observations in favor of conclusions supported by relatively few apparently counter observations.

3

Delineating the Field

Justice and injustice do not exist in relation to beings who have not been able to make a compact with the object of avoiding mutual harm.

—Epicurus

Let us suppose that nature has bestowed on the human race such profuse *abundance* of all *external* conveniences, that, . . . every individual finds himself fully provided with whatever his . . . luxurious imagination wish or desire. . . . It seems evident that, in such a happy state, every other social virtue would flourish, . . . but the cautious, jealous virtue of justice would never once have been dreamed of. For what purpose make a partition of goods, where every one has already more than enough? . . . Why call this *mine,* when upon the seizing of it by another, I need but stretch out my hand to possess myself of what is equally valuable? Justice, in that case, being totally useless, would be an idle ceremonial, and could never possibly have a place in the catalogue of virtues.

—David Hume

The theory that all altruistic sentiments and desires evolved because of the genetic benefits yielded by reciprocal or kin altruism suggests that one or another, or both, of these kinds of sentiments are the ones that merit the label of *moral.* What then are these feelings? Love, affection, empathy, shame, guilt, embarrassment, the desire to be loyal, to keep promises, to benefit close kin and friends, not to cheat or deceive others, and so on.

Yet there are significant differences between the sentiments related to reciprocal and to kin altruism. The love felt for offspring is not the same as that directed towards mates, lovers, or friends, with whom we have reciprocal arrangements.[1] These differences can be explained in terms of the genetic benefits of the altruistic practices that generate them. Reciprocal altruistic practices typically endure only when they yield *mutual benefit*. When that is lacking, the urge towards reciprocity declines or evaporates. Marriages dissolve, friends part, contracts are not renewed. Kin-altruistic practices, on the other hand, tend to endure in the absence of mutual benefit. Parents nourish offspring whether they expect reciprocity or not. Unrequited love felt for friends or marriage partners tends to fade, but love for kin, at least of the kind felt by parents for offspring, is of a hardier variety.

There is another difference between reciprocal and kin altruism that merits attention. It often is the case that, having already received the benefits of another party's altruism and being able to defect with impunity, we come through with the goods anyway. This sometimes is true even when we have no desire whatever to benefit the other parties or, worse, hate their guts. We do so not from a desire to benefit them but because of a feeling of *obligation*. Kin altruism is different. It typically is engaged in without regard to feelings of obligation. We do kin-altruistic acts, in particular those directed towards offspring, because *we desire their benefit*. The benefit to us is obtained only indirectly in the satisfaction of our desire for their welfare.

It is these differences that make plausible restricting the label *moral* to sentiments, desires, and behavior of a reciprocal altruistic nature. It seems more to the point to speak of an *obligation* when one has made a promise, say, to a business associate, than when one has acted altruistically towards children. In the former case, every motive other than a desire to play the game straight may incline one to renege; in the latter case, the altruistic behavior is motivated primarily by a desire to benefit close kin. Note also that in the case of promise keeping, the feeling of obligation is one of owing others, of accepting their demand for reciprocity, whereas in the case of benefiting offspring, the feeling is of wanting to do so irrespective of their thoughts on the matter.

But the point is not the rightness or wrongness of affixing the label

---

[1]While the reciprocity in matehood is obvious, it sometimes is overlooked that friendship also is based on reciprocity and that friendships tend to dissolve into something else when they become overly one-sided or provide no benefits for one or both parties. Friendship and its relationship to morality are discussed further in chapter 6.

moral just to reciprocal-altruistic behavior. The point is to pay attention to the fundamental differences between the two kinds of altruism just mentioned. There is no mistake in saying that one has an obligation to benefit one's offspring provided it is seen that this is a different sort of obligation than arises from having entered into reciprocal arrangements. The concept of obligation is not made in heaven. There are ways in which most of the tugs often thought of as moral resemble each other and ways in which they are different. Understanding their resemblances and differences is what counts, not knowing which of them "really" are moral and which are not.

Of course, denying the existence of obligations towards offspring qua offspring does not entail that we have no obligations towards them whatsoever. Parents can enter into agreements with their own children just as with anyone else. Indeed, living in close proximity almost guarantees that they will do so quite frequently. In addition, agreements can be, and generally are, made with others concerning the care of offspring. Every culture needs to make agreements, written or unwritten, explicit or implicit, concerning the raising of the next generation, in particular because everyone in a society has an interest in the general quality of its members (at the very least because of competition with outgroups). In most societies, these agreements place the primary care of children in the hands of their parents (or close kin), because only they are motivated by kin-altruistic as well as reciprocal-altruistic motives to do the job satisfactorily. So in most cultures, parents do have an obligation towards their children, but this obligation is generated by agreements, implicit or explicit, and not automatically because of a parent-child genetic relationship.

The central idea of this chapter is that evolution theory points to *promises* (agreements, contracts) as the factor that generates moral obligations. But does this fit with what introspection has to say about the matter? There can be no single answer to this question, in particular because intuitions differ from person to person. But it is clear that, for most of us at any rate, our intuitions are strong that in straightforward cases promising does bind a person to compliance. The more interesting issue is whether typical human sentiments favor the idea that there are moral obligations not generated by contractual arrangements—obligations requiring us to be charitable towards the poor or to take good care of our own children. There can be little doubt that most of us do look down on self-centered, selfish people who lack compassion for the downtrodden, and do regard those who seriously neglect their own offspring as defective, *bad* human beings. The question is whether we want to say that every bad person is therefore *immoral*. In other words, do we want to say that there is a special obligation to be charitable, or to take care of offspring? On the view being espoused here, there are good reasons, provided above, for not speaking in this way. (See also chapter 17 on the good, as opposed to the moral, person.)

4

Fair Contract Fundamentals

[M]ay the better participant emerge triumphant.
— Ring announcer (Harry Balogh?)
at a Joe Louis championship bout

Whatsoever ye sow, ye also *ought* to reap.
— Variation on a biblical precept

Profitable cooperation is an important ingredient required for the development of a sense of fair play. But it alone is not sufficient. Bees, ants, and the other social insects are cooperators par excellence with relevant in-group members (members of the same caste who are, in effect, clones of each other), yet they do not develop practices of fair play because there is no genetic benefit to be gained from *competition* with genetically identical fellows. (Ants do compete with ants in other ant hills, with whom they are not genetically related. But there is no benefit in cooperating with them, and so no fair play practices have developed between competing ant hills.)

Human beings, unlike these other animals, have developed a sense of fair play because, as stressed before, they must cooperate with each other in order to survive and procreate and yet are each other's most serious genetic competitors. It is this combination of cooperator/competitor that is required for the development of a sense of fairness.

There are essentially two kinds of fair agreements, concerning fair cooperation and fair competition respectively. Although sentiments on the matter are not precise by any means, the key to an understanding of the concept of cooperative fairness is that those who regularly fail to get at least their fair share of the fruits of cooperative ventures tend to lose out in the genetic proliferation game to craftier competitors. Contributing more to a cooperative venture but benefiting less typically worsens a person's competitive position vis-à-vis those who contribute less but receive more. The genetic point is that relative gain often counts more than absolute gain. (The desire to keep up with the Joneses, or better yet, to get ahead of them, thus is not without its biological underpinnings.) That is why an agreement is generally thought to be *cooperatively fair* only if it divides the fruits of a common venture according to the amount of effective effort, time, goods, knowledge, and so on, each person contributes to it. When every party makes an identical contribution, fairness thus requires an equal division of the resulting profits; when some contribute more, fairness requires that they receive a larger share than those who contribute less.

The genetic importance of getting at least one's fair share explains why most human beings have at least a modestly good sense of what counts as a fair share and why we try so hard to make sure that we don't get the short end of the stick. Note, by the way, that knowing what constitutes a fair share is just as vital to the sharp operator intent on obtaining a greater than fair share as it is to the honest person who just doesn't want to be taken. Most cheating involves not out-and-out thievery but just stacking the deck in one's favor, and criminals need to know when the deck *is* stacked in their favor.[1]

An agreement is generally seen to be *competitively fair* only if its terms do not favor a particular competitor—only if they do not provide an advantage to any competing party. The rules governing most sporting events, for instance, are deliberately constructed so that this is the case. Indeed, to the extent that the rules of a game do yield an advantage to one competitor or another, they tend not to be considered sporting.[2]

The unsporting nature of competitively unfair games points to the reason that our keen sense of competitive fairness has evolved. Clearly, those who uncomplainingly engage in activities that are rigged against them will tend to be genetic losers.

---

[1]This suggests a point neglected in the previous chapter where the moral sentiments were tied primarily to the cooperative and altruistic side of human nature. The need not to be taken in by competitors when the spoils of cooperative ventures are divided no doubt accounts in part for the evolution of our sense as to what counts as a fair share.

[2]The important exceptions to this idea are hunting, fishing, and bull fighting, contests between human beings and other animals. Why these should be thought of as sports is something this writer is unable to comprehend.

Of course, life being what it is, we frequently are forced to compete when the rules favor other competitors or when we have to accept less than a fair share of the spoils or none at all. When the choice is either being shut out of the game or accepting a smaller than fair share, prudence dictates doing the best we can under the circumstances and living to try again another day. But it almost always is *better* to have at least a fair chance at success and to obtain at least a fair share of the fruits of cooperative efforts.

In general, it's easier to specify fair rules for competitive than for cooperative enterprises, because so many rules that treat every competitor in the same way, whatever that way happens to be, turn out to be fair. But this isn't always the case. A rule requiring Olympic marathon runners to wear shoes would deal equally with every competitor and yet could be seen as unfair to runners who compete best bare-footed, as did one outstanding Olympic marathon champion. Similarly, a rule requiring that economic and political activities in Canada be conducted in English would treat every Canadian equally but no doubt would be regarded as unfair by the French-speaking citizens of Quebec. (The underlying problem these examples bring to the fore is discussed further in chapter 7.)

But the difficulties encountered in trying to specify rules for fairness in cooperative ventures are of a different sort. The division of labor, the accumulation and investment of capital, and the increasing complexity of modern cooperative organizations have produced ventures in which the kinds and amounts of effective effort, goods provided, and so on, differ greatly from member to member. How are the contributions of an assembly line worker to be compared with those of middle or higher management, or with investors who provide capital? That these are difficult questions on which everyone cannot be expected to agree does not mean that they are meaningless, or to be avoided. It does mean, however, that they cannot be answered once and for all, by philosophers or by anyone else. (Some of the relevant complexities will nevertheless be discussed later in chapter 15.)

Of course, competitive and cooperative fairness are not always, or even usually, separate items. In the extremely important case of competition for mates, wealth gained via cooperative ventures frequently plays a significant or even decisive role in deciding who wins (in virtually every culture, the rich attract mates much more readily than do the poor). So when wealth is gained by an unfair distribution of the fruits of cooperative efforts, this unfairness then infuses what might otherwise have been a fair competition for mates. Similar remarks apply to other sorts of competitive activities.

In any case, once an agreement has been reached, our sense of fairness urges us to live up to it, provided reciprocity can be expected. But there is no overarching moral principle requiring us to make agreements about anything. Prudence usually dictates that we do so, but that is another matter.

Before turning to other matters, three points need to be stressed. First, not all agreements are of the explicit variety. Custom, for example, often generates agreements that are binding even though implicit. Most social obligations—to wear appropriate dress when in public, to aid fellow citizens in distress—tend to arise in this way and only later, if at all, are put into so many words.

Second, fairness, in philosophical lingo, is a relational concept. For example, if, in return for important favors, Smith promises a unique coin both to Jones and to Brown and then gives it to Jones, it follows that Smith has been fair to Jones but not to Brown. It makes no sense to say either that Smith acted fairly or that he didn't; he treated Jones fairly but not Brown. (Notice also that on the theory being espoused here, the famous dictum *ought implies can* has to be rejected. Smith ought to give the coin both to Jones and to Brown, but he *cannot* do so.)

Third, fair play is not generally thought to require us to live up to *coerced* agreements. We don't feel obligated, for example, to keep a promise made under threat of death. But *advantage takings* are another matter (to be dealt with later, in particular in chapter 6 where friendly and unfriendly kinds of competition are discussed).

5

Retribution, Restitution, Revenge

Few are those who expire never having lusted to revenge betrayal.
—Harold Gordon

. . . an eye for an eye and tooth for a tooth.
—Old Testament

Don't get mad, get *even*.
—Old saying

Human beings keep fair bargains for essentially three sorts of reasons: the prospect of personal gain, a sense of fair play that moderates the temptation to defect, and fear of being caught and punished. To increase the likelihood that sinners will in fact be caught *and punished,* nature has evolved in us a sense of retribution, a desire to strike back at those who cheat.

Controversies concerning retribution tend to be clouded by the vagueness and ambiguity surrounding this concept and its neighbors, restitution and revenge. By *restitution* we mean here the act of restoring the balance of fair competition that an unfair action has destroyed. This is generally accomplished by taking away the transgressor's advantage or by restoring the loss to the party harmed. If Smith steals from Jones, restitution requires that the items stolen, or comparable goods, be taken from Smith and given back to Jones. Restitution restores fairness to the competitive marketplace but does not inflict a penalty on those who were unfair. Requiring that a sprinter who jumps the gun return to the starting line thus constitutes restitution because it restores fair competition among the runners.

Restitution is usually regarded as sufficient when there is no deliberate attempt to transgress, or the transgressor's intent cannot be determined, or (sometimes) when there is good evidence of remorse or the likelihood of reform.

By *retribution,* we mean here the harming of offenders in return for their misconduct so that they are less well off afterwards than before. A strong desire for retribution, for a penalty that constitutes genuine punishment, almost certainly evolved because of its deterring effect on deliberate transgressions. Simply requiring those who cheat to return their plunder makes crime a highly profitable activity, given that not every foul deed is discovered and rectified. A harsher penalty than mere restitution is required, and nature seems to have given us a rather strong desire that it be inflicted.

Notice, however, that deterrence frequently is not our principal motive, or even a motive at all, when we punish wrongdoers. This is true in particular when heinous acts have aroused our anger. Evidence for this is the fact that we have a strong desire to obtain retribution in cases where deterrence (not to mention rehabilitation) is either impossible or extremely unlikely. We thus punished the leaders of Germany and Japan after World War II even though history attests to the unlikelihood that aspiring tyrants can be deterred in this way. Punishing the guilty in these cases generates a feeling akin to catharsis, a feeling that justice has been done. Similarly, when we read about heinous crimes committed centuries ago, it is satisfying to learn that the guilty were punished, but we feel dismay if they were not, even though, obviously, there is no possibility of deterrence or rehabilitation at this late date.

It should be clear then that there is a strong sentiment favoring retribution quite separate from the desire to deter sin, even though retributive sentiments almost certainly evolved because they increased the likelihood of deterrence (just as there is a strong desire for sex independent of the desire for offspring, even though sexual desire without doubt evolved because it increased the likelihood of reproduction).

By *revenge* we mean here the infliction of a harm in return for being harmed. This means that the concepts of revenge and of retribution overlap; some cases of revenge constitute retribution and some (particularly when guilty parties strike back at their punishers) do not.

Virtually everyone sees revenge that does not also constitute retribution as odious, but opinions divide sharply concerning retributive revenge. One reason for this difference of opinion may be that some of the foulness of nonretributive cases has become attached in some minds to those that are retributive. Another, perhaps, stems from the feelings of empathy it is natural to have for all human beings, indeed to some extent for all sentient beings, that mask retributive sentiments. Still another is that we often punish in order to deter or rehabilitate, and this too tends to make us overlook a concurrent desire for retribution. Note also that we find the punishment of *innocent* victims abhorrent even in cases when it would have great deterring effect.[1]

There also are several other reasons, rather difficult to specify, for the denial of natural retributive yearnings. One is the occasional need to present a positive, non-vindictive persona to society at large; in time this may lead to the repression of retributive sentiments, and thus to their conscious denial.[2] Another is the desire not to be punished for our own sins; if others who are guilty ought to be punished, then so should we. (Interestingly, there is a strong, often unconscious, counterforce to this sentiment in most of us that sometimes pushes us to *demand* punishment for our own serious crimes.)[3]

Finally, we often have desires or fears which conflict with our desire for retribution. Cheated by others, we sometimes find legal redress too costly. Having been robbed, extorted from, or raped, we often fail to give testimony out of fear of retaliation or to avoid humiliation.

There are many theorists, of course, who see the natural human desire for retribution as merely a vestige of our tooth and claw origins, always to be fought against, not satisfied. But this quick dismissal is a mistake. After all, similar remarks can be made about all normal human sentiments, including the ones that incline some theorists to see retribution as odious. The rational person fights against desires only when

---

[1]One of the textbook objections to some versions of utilitarianism is that in certain cases it requires the punishment of innocent parties if doing so will have a deterrent effect. Some writers have proposed mixed deterrent/retribution theories to overcome this objection. One such theory would have us punish the guilty only when doing so will have a deterrent effect but never punish those who are innocent for that purpose. See, for instance, Jerry Cederbloom, "The Retributive Liability Theory of Punishment." *Public Affairs Quarterly* 9:4, 1995.

[2]Note that those theoretically committed to nonviolence frequently succumb to retributive urges in the heat of passion.

[3]In "Persons and Punishment," a fascinating article appearing in *The Monist* 52:4 (October 1968):475–501, and reprinted in Joel Feinberg and Hyman Gross, eds., *Philosophy of Law* (Belmont, Calif.: Wadsworth Publishing Co., 1975), Herbert Morris argues for the related point that we have a right to be punished for our crimes.

their satisfaction is likely to conflict with the overall satisfaction of other desires, and it is clear that this likelihood only sometimes exists with respect to the desire for retribution.

Earlier in this chapter, we characterized retribution as the harming of offenders in return for their misconduct so that they are less well off afterwards than before. While accurate as far as it goes, this way of looking at retribution needs augmentation. In particular, we need to add the idea, implicit in the saying "The punishment should fit the crime," that more serious infringements should be punished more heavily than those of lesser moment. Requiring that someone who inflicts serious bodily injury in the act of theft be divested of the stolen goods plus, say, a fifty-dollar fine, renders the criminal worse off than before but does not yield justice, because the fifty-dollar penalty does not reflect the seriousness of the felony. The complete price of retribution has not been paid. The reason for this is that to be biologically successful, retribution must assure that wrongdoers do not gain a competitive advantage over those they have wronged (or anyone else for that matter). A penalty of fifty dollars in the case in question, while it harms the thief's competitive position relative to some others, may still leave the thief with a competitive advantage over the person harmed. Perfect retribution thus requires restitution, as well as appropriate harm to the offender, so that the competitive position of the criminal is worsened while that of the victim is not.

Of course, in some cases, murder and rape perhaps providing the best examples, restitution is not possible. This may be one reason, aside from the enormity of these crimes, that it generally is believed punishment should be severe when these crimes are committed. Indeed, these crimes may well be seen as so heinous at least in part because of the impossibility of restoring the balance by restitution. When we make things additionally worse for the sinner (or, in some cases, when we provide restitution to a victim's heirs), we do our best to make up for our failure to provide the victim with restitution.

We also commonly inflict much harsher penalties for deliberate killings than for those done accidentally. The crime in the case of accidental killings is negligence (note that the crime is generally referred to as *negligent* homicide) whereas deliberate killings are thought of as murder. Yet in both kinds of cases, the harms inflicted are the same. What is different is the way we feel about the perpetrators. Similarly, we distinguish between killings that are planned ahead of time and those committed in the heat of passion, and we assign a lesser penalty to the latter even though the intent is the same in both cases. Again, the difference has to do with the way we feel about the cold-blooded killer as compared to the person who kills in the heat of passion.

Further, in assessing penalties for crimes, psychological factors concerning remorse, character, intentions, and motives are generally thought to be relevant. The reason is not just that we are concerned with deterrence and rehabilitation, but also that, contrary to the popular slogan, we tend to hate the criminal at least as much as the crime, and in proportion to the nastiness of the transgression (murderers and rapists being seen as a good deal more odious than pickpockets and ordinary con artists).

The difference that makes the difference in each of the cases just considered is the state of mind of the offender. The deliberate killer has a mind-set that is more likely to lead to further crimes than someone who kills accidentally, out of negligence, or in the heat of passion. A person who suffers genuine remorse is more likely to play the game straight in the future than someone who feels no guilt. Nature instills degrees of hatred in us that roughly mirror these facts, leading us to feel greater animosity towards cold-blooded criminals than the less guilty-minded and motivating us, therefore, to punish the former more harshly.[4] Of course, we do sometimes inflict greater harms for reasons of deterrence (it generally takes the threat posed by a severe penalty to deter cold-blooded criminals), but that is another matter.

Interestingly, in the twentieth century, another sort of case concerning intentions and motives, previously smoldering in the background, has come to the fore because science now has provided us with a modestly good understanding of the role the unconscious plays in human behavior. Negligent homicide, to take one example, sometimes occurs simply because someone is forgetful, or preoccupied with other matters, but it also may occur because the unconscious mind makes sure sufficient care is not taken. Should unconsciously motivated negligent homicide be thought of as murder? Should we sometimes hate those who commit crimes through negligence as much as those who do so with conscious intent?

On the one hand, there is the feeling that only conscious awareness at the crucial moment should count in assessing intent. On the other,

---

[4]One of the problems with the biblical principle of an eye for an eye and a tooth for a tooth is that when taken literally, it fails to consider the state of mind of an offender, treating, for example, merely negligent transgressors in the same way as the more cold-blooded variety.

there is the idea that unconsciously motivated acts reflect character just as much as those that are consciously motivated, an idea supported by the fact that we often become conscious of the hidden intent later, well after the nasty deed has been done. Given the modern understanding that most actions are at least partly unconsciously motivated, anyone who believes that human beings should in general be held accountable for their actions has to conclude that this applies to those whose motivations are unconscious as well as conscious. (Unfortunately, the two underlying issues here—the psychological one concerning the role played by unconscious motivation and the philosophical one of free will versus determinism—are beyond the scope of this work, although it should be clear from what has been said where the sympathies of this writer rest.)

Friendships and Degrees of Friendliness

Every one must have noticed how miserable horses, dogs, sheep, &c., are when separated from their companions, and what strong mutual affection the two former kinds, at least, shew on their re-union. It is curious to speculate on the feelings of a dog, who will rest peacefully for hours in a room with his master or any of his family, without the least notice being taken of him; but if left for a short time by himself, barks or howls dismally.

—Charles Darwin

I like George Bush very much but I disagree with him when he talks of a kinder, gentler America. I think if this country gets any kinder or gentler, it's literally going to cease to exist.

—Donald Trump (hard-nosed entrepreneur)

A friend in deed is a friend indeed.

—Variously attributed

Cosmus, Duke of Florence, was wont to say of perfidious friends, that "We read that we ought to forgive our enemies; but we do not read that we ought to forgive our friends."

—Francis Bacon

Friends form a kind of small in-group within or overlapping larger in-groups, including the primary ones that we think of as constituting societies. Indeed, societies can be thought of as very large groups of friends, although, of course, friends who on average are not nearly as friendly as two people often are.

Other things being equal, groups of friends will tend to win out when pitted against groups held together only by prospects of personal gain, and this may well be the reason for the evolution of feelings of group loyalty that cement friendships and make for the kind of close-knit groups we think of as societies.

The more, and the more important, the cooperative behavior engaged in by associations of any kind, the greater their *degree* of friendliness, other things being equal. But merely engaging in cooperative behavior, no matter how extensively, does not make an association into a friendship, or a group into a society. Criminals frequently cooperate with each other, as do competing businesses, and even warring societies often cooperate by agreeing to limit fighting in one way or another. The point is that increases in cooperative behavior among *friends,* or among the members of a *society,* tend to increase the degree of friendliness of such an association, although cooperation alone does not necessarily do so.

What is lacking in the case of nonfriends who cooperate is a reciprocity of concern for the other party that leads to an increase in trustworthiness (fidelity, loyalty, honesty), a decrease in advantage taking (profiting from another's unfortunate circumstances or lack of knowledge, strength, intelligence, wealth, etc.), and a willingness to come to each other's aid in time of need or when assistance is likely to yield a significantly greater benefit to the recipient than it does cost to the benefactor. Enemies cooperate solely for their own advantage; friends do so also out of a sense of concern and loyalty.

Yet friends, no matter how close, sometimes are competitors (for jobs, sex partners, mates, political power, fame, etc.), one reason that there are no completely true friends (the point of Aristotle's remark, "Ah, my friends, there are no friends"). Extremely hard-nosed competition between friends, in particular for mates or for positions of power, usually strains friendships to the breaking point.

Other things being equal, the gentler competition between friends, the greater the degree of friendliness between them. Similarly, the greater the sacrifices friends are willing to make for each other, the greater the degree of their friendliness. In effect, friends provide insurance to each other, paid for by the reciprocity of their willingness to come to each other's aid. There are, of course, limits to how far even the closest friends are willing to go for each other, due to the fact that we all value our own welfare more than that of anyone else (with the possible occasional exception of offspring or other close kin).

Given that societies constitute rather large groups of friends, citizens are generally expected to come to each other's aid in certain ways. However, not being as close on average as full-fledged friends, citizens have duties to each other that are relatively limited compared to those of close friends, usually just requiring us to behave in public in a civil manner, provide directions to strangers, toss lines to drowning fellows, and so on.[1] When this and other sorts of friendliness diminish beyond a certain point, disaffection increases and loyalties fade, just as true friendships disintegrate when they become too one-sided or fail to benefit one party or another.

Because friendliness is so useful in generating the benefits of increases in cooperative behavior, it often is mistaken for fairness. But the two are somewhat different. We all are familiar with mean spirited (unfriendly), sour people who nevertheless are scrupulously fair minded. So in theory, a completely fair society need not be very friendly (a point to be discussed further in chapter 9). Nevertheless, it isn't always easy to distinguish friendliness from fair play, in particular because it may come down to a question of which competitive games we wish to play (a point to be discussed in the next chapter).

Throughout history, societies have differed widely with respect to degrees of friendliness. In the United States today, for instance, most kinds of insider trading are considered crimes, as are the obtaining of money under false pretenses and the selling of contaminated food. Until quite recently, however, the rule in America was *caveat emptor* — let the buyer beware.[2] This doesn't mean the system in America is fairer today than in times past. But it does mean that it is friendlier.

Note, by the way, that these remarks about taking advantage of another's ignorance apply also to other sorts of advantage takings, even to extreme cases when natural disasters have struck. That most of us find it odious to sell water at one hundred dollars a gallon when hurricanes foul normal supplies proves only that we prefer friendlier sorts of economic practices, not that a system which permits this sort of meanness is automatically unfair.

We also shouldn't conclude too hastily that increases in friendliness

---

[1]Duties of this sort are fewer, and less demanding, in the large, diverse nations of the modern world than they are in most small, cohesive hunting-and-gathering societies, reflecting the unfortunately less friendly nature of the former compared to the latter. Indeed, the desirability of friendliness constitutes a serious reason for preferring small to large societies.

[2]There were no laws against commercial misrepresentation in England until 1757. In 1703, in the trial of a man who had masqueraded as a creditor's agent, an English Lord Chief Justice instructed a jury with the then commonsense thought, "Shall we indict one man for making a fool of another?"

will always be seen as desirable by everyone. Some temperaments thrive on less friendliness rather than more. The business world and political arenas are full of people who enjoy the freedom to fleece the ignorant or foolish and who prefer games in which everyone has to be on guard against sharp practices. The principle of *caveat emptor* suits their competitive urges very well. (Recall the remark by Donald Trump quoted at the beginning of this chapter.) Nor should we conclude automatically that these people are less fair-minded than those who desire a greater degree of friendliness (although it may well be that many of them are). As we have been at some pains to suggest, unfriendliness and fair-mindedness are not in themselves antithetical. They are, of course, when the paucity of friendliness results from dishonesty. But being fair-minded does not require softness of competition.

Nevertheless, friendly societies have an advantage over the more hard-nosed variety, and tend to win out when competing against them, just as fairer groups tend to defeat the less fair. When buyers must beware, transactions consume much more time and effort, and general productivity is reduced. When sellers cannot trust buyers to pay up, the benefits of delayed reciprocal transactions tend to be lost. Being taken in by deceptive practices tends to make those fleeced more inclined to play similarly nasty and thus costly games. Litigation and unproductive paper work increase. Honesty and fair play decrease.

So even though there is no contradiction in the concept of an unfriendly but fair-minded individual, in the real world friendliness tends to increase cooperation in general and fair cooperation in particular, because it increases the likelihood that bargains will be lived up to and decreases the incidence of outright theft and other sorts of uncooperative interactions. Friendliness, like fair play, thus renders societies safer for the grudging reciprocity that generates most of the benefits of human social existence.

7

The Impartiality of Competitive Rules

The law, in its majestic equality, forbids rich and poor alike to
sleep under bridges, beg in the streets or steal bread.

— Anatole France

As remarked in chapter 4, competitive rules are fair only if they do not
favor the chances of some competitors over others, so that, barring
chance or accidents, better performers win. But when is it better performance and not the competitive rules themselves that determine victory?

Take the football rule change, made soon after World War II, that
permitted unlimited substitutions. Although the new rule favors teams
better stocked with specialists while the old favored all-around players
and those having great endurance, we think of the new and old rules as
equally fair. We do so because the talents and skills favored by the new
are thought of as equally relevant to the game we wish to see played as
are those favored by the old.

On the other hand, consider the earlier change in National Football
League rules that required all teams to play the same number of games
at home as away rather than, as previously, having more games played
before large constituencies than before small. We regard this change as
having increased the fairness of the games because we don't think the
"talent" favored by the old rule (representing a larger constituency) is
relevant to the game of football; the new rule increased the likelihood
that those who more effectively employed the relevant talent would
"emerge triumphant."

Unfortunately, there is no automatic, or easy, way to decide whether
the rules of a game do or don't favor some competitors over others. Take
the two football rule changes just considered. We see the change allowing unlimited player substitution as neither increasing nor decreasing the

fairness of football rules because it simply changes the talents required in the players themselves. The rule change requiring that the same number of games be played both at home as away, on the other hand, is perceived as increasing the fairness of the game because the talent it disfavors, a home field advantage, is not one intrinsic to the players themselves.

But this doesn't always work. Consider the competition between two males for the hand of a female. We don't think that this sort of contest automatically is unfair when the talent that tips the scales in favor of the winning suitor happens to be having greater wealth than his rival, a talent external to the suitor himself. We don't think that the winner has competed unfairly by making his wealth known to the woman being courted. In this case, we see the external "talent" of having greater wealth as relevant to the competition between males for females. Whether a talent is internal or external does count in deciding questions of fairness, but it isn't necessarily overriding.

Sometimes, in fact, what makes a talent relevant or irrelevant is a matter of taste, of which talents we admire or enjoy seeing in action. We admire the kinds of internal skills that make for winning football (speed, dexterity, presence of mind) and enjoy seeing them honed close to perfection, whereas the external talent, say, of representing a large constituency leaves us cold.[1] In other cases, it is practical considerations that move us to regard talents as relevant or irrelevant. We tend not to require equality of external talents as a condition of fair competition when practical matters make it out of the question to do so, as in competitions between suitors.

The point of all this is simply that there is no easy way to decide which talents should be counted as relevant in determining the fairness or unfairness of particular games. In each case, inevitably, decisions will be influenced by practical considerations and by matters of taste.

---

[1]Intuitions differ among theoreticians concerning the talents that should be rewarded in the games played in everyday life. For instance, in his book *A Theory of Justice* (Cambridge: Harvard University Press, 1971), John Rawls argues that wealth obtained in the marketplace by virtue of superior natural talents, such as intelligence, is not deserved, one reason, we may presume, that he opts for his more or less egalitarian principle of distributive justice. (To be consistent, he ought to argue, as he doesn't, for a similar amount of egalitarianism in the distribution of the power and recognition that also and equally stem from natural talents such as intelligence, drive, and charisma.) By way of contrast, many contractual theorists, including this writer, see talents such as intelligence as very relevant indeed to the competitions of everyday life. We like the idea that, say, smarter competitors in the business world tend to win out over those who are less intelligent.

It also needs to be noticed that merely wanting a game to be played, say for practical reasons, does not automatically make us think that the talents determining winners and losers are relevant to its fairness or unfairness. We may want a game to be played even though it is perceived as being unfair (a point to be expanded on in chapter 10 where unfair but desirable outcomes are discussed).

Also note that intuitions concerning fairness tend to be uncertain with respect to some of the most important competitions in everyday life. Is the stock-trading game unfair because it does not require all players to start with the same amount of capital, or is it fair because wealth is a relevant external talent? That practical considerations preclude requiring every stock trader to start with the same amount of funds tends to make us see wealth as a relevant talent. However, most of us are moved in the other direction by the realization that having lots of money is an external talent and thus is unlike, say, the talent of understanding how human greed, or the herd instinct, or new scientific discoveries, will influence stock prices. (Interestingly, in the case of poker, a much less vital game than those played on stock markets, championship competitions that attempt to be as fair as possible require all players to start with the same number of chips.)

Finally, note that considerations of game fairness sometimes are related to questions as to when it is a particular game that is being played and not a similar but nevertheless different one. Usually, the matter is easily decided, as in the case of singles and doubles tennis (thought of, perhaps, as separate games because of their different rules concerning court size and number of players). There are many cases, though, that are not so quickly or easily decided, and in which questions of fairness intrude.

The game of professional baseball, for example, has changed a good deal over the years, and yet we apply the same name to all of the various (hardball) versions. One reason for this is that we want to compare the old heroes and their records with the new. We want to be able to say that Pete Rose broke Ty Cobb's lifetime hit record, not that Rose holds the "live baseball" and Cobb the "dead baseball" record. But questions of fairness may lead to hedging: we may want to have our cake (calling slightly different games by the same name) while eating it too (distinguishing between them for the sake of fair play). We want to think of Roger Maris and Babe Ruth as having both played something called "major league baseball," so that we can compare their records, but we also want to be fair to Ruth when we say that Maris broke Ruth's single-season home run record. We do this by placing an asterisk before a listing of Maris's record to indicate that his great season consisted of 162 games and not the 154 in which Babe Ruth set the previous record.[2] (Note the similarity of these examples to age-old philosophical conundrums like the one about whether, when we have replaced every part of a ship, the resulting item is or isn't the same as the original. In the ship example, we tend to say *yes,* or *no,* depending on "external" factors, for instance, on who we want to have legal title to the reconstructed item. The point is that there are no "correct" answers independent of such extraneous considerations.)

---

[2]Interestingly, those in charge of these matters recently decided, unfairly it seems to this baseball fan, to remove the asterisk from Maris's record.

8

Fair Group Decision Procedures

One man, one vote.
> —Traditional principle of justice

One person, one vote.
> —Recent emendation of traditional principle of justice

As stated earlier, competitive rules are fair only when they do not favor some players over others. Since coming to agreement is a competitive activity (the various parties all want their ways of doing things to be chosen), procedures for reaching agreement are fair only if they grant each participant an equal say in the decision process. The point of *Robert's Rules of Order* is precisely to assure this kind of procedural fairness in legislative arenas. (Note, by the way, that *Robert's Rules* are perceived to be fair by peoples all over the world, a fact that reinforces the claim made earlier concerning the existence of a universal sense of fair play underlying the diversity of norms existing in different cultures.)

It often is thought that unanimity is the only completely fair group decision procedure. (Indeed, this writer once thought so himself.) But that isn't the case. What makes a group decision procedure fair is just that it treats all participants equally. A rule specifying a simple majority, or even a mere plurality, satisfies this requirement as well as a rule requiring unanimity.

Interestingly, there are many small social groups, and a few small societies, in which complete unanimity is strived for and, in most cases, obtained, before actions are taken. Members of these groups discuss matters until, usually after a good deal of give and take, all agree on a course of action. This does not mean, of course, that all truly believe the chosen path is the best one, but rather that dissenters become persuaded to accept the favored course in the interests of group harmony and solidarity, and also because the benefits likely to flow from adoption of the winning plan are greater than can be obtained in the absence of any agreement at all. Group decision procedures requiring less than unanimity are similar in that they constitute methods for groups to select from the various possible courses of actions the ones to be given unanimous support. Instead of talking or browbeating until unanimity is achieved, votes are taken after a certain amount of debate, and the victorious measures are then accepted by all. Voting becomes a device for achieving unanimity.

Because practicality forces large groups to elect officers, thus granting some members greater power over choices than others, it may be thought that practical decision procedures for large groups cannot be genuinely fair. But fairness is possible if those granted greater power are themselves chosen by fair procedures. Similarly, although some group members inevitably win greater power through the force of their personalities, intelligence, or oratorical or political skills, that does not reflect against the fairness of a procedural rule if these personal talents are considered to be relevant to the group decision game.

Of course, the mere fairness of a procedure does not guarantee a fair outcome. For one thing, human intelligence is not infallible. For another, human nature is not completely altruistic. Members of a group typically will cast votes partly, indeed generally largely, on the basis of self-interest.[1] (It is true, however, that procedural fairness makes tyranny less likely and that the closer a group moves towards a requirement of unanimity, the more difficult it is for some to take advantage of others.)

Finally, note that the same problems encountered before concerning relevant talents arise when trying to specify fair decision procedures. Simply requiring that each person have only one vote and that, say, a majority always rules, leaves open the possibility that votes will be won by means of threats or bribes. If, say, the ability to bribe others is considered a relevant talent when playing the decision procedure game, then the Rockefellers of the world will tend to win elections (as in fact they do) and get their legislation accepted, while poor folks will have fewer prospects. Members of an extremely unfriendly society could, of course, consciously opt for such a system, and it would be fair if (contrary to the actual case in virtually every existing society) everyone had an equal opportunity to accumulate the required wealth.

---

[1]One of the points James S. Fishkin makes in his book *Tyranny and Legitimacy* (Baltimore: Johns Hopkins University Press, 1979) is that no procedure can guarantee the elimination of tyrannical outcomes.

Nations (Societies) and Governments

Man is by nature a social animal. . . . Anyone who either cannot lead the common life or is so self-sufficient as not to need to, and therefore does not partake of society, is either a beast or he is a god.
—Aristotle

No man is an island.
—John Donne

The non-social individual is an abstraction arrived at by imagining what man would be if all his human qualities were taken away . . . . Society, as a real whole, is the normal order, and the mass as an aggregate of isolated units is the fiction.
—John Dewey

Nations (societies, cultures) are specimens of that special kind of club anthropologists think of as *in-groups*. (Families constitute another species of the genus.) In-groups hark back to mankind's dim primate past, and an understanding of the strong urge most of us have to belong to and be loyal to an in-group is crucial to an understanding of the moral side of human life.

Nations differ from ordinary clubs in several important ways. In particular, their rules and customs take precedence in the public arena over those of every other group. Nations are *sovereign*. (But note that within the private arena of the family, blood loyalty frequently takes precedence.) Pledging allegiance to a primary in-group is one of the fundamental things that we human beings do, indeed must do if we are to lead satisfying lives. We become members of a particular national in-group at birth and generally are granted the full rights and obligations of citizenship upon reaching maturity. Voluntarily leaving our native society requires entering another and tends to be an extremely traumatic last-resort act. (Until recently, being forced into exile usually was a catastrophe.) The customs and regulations of our primary in-group are already largely in place when we arrive on the scene and must be accepted, more or less, as a condition of citizenship. Most other groups are quite different in that membership is not automatic, leaving entails no great trauma, and alternative groups are easily found. (The one exception, of course, is the familial in-group; rejecting one's family also generally involves great trauma, and joining another family, as in the case of acquiring foster parents, is not quite the same thing.)

Nevertheless, nations don't differ from other kinds of clubs with respect to matters of fairness. A society's competitive rules, just as those of other kinds of groups, are fair only if they do not favor particular members over others; its cooperative rules are fair only if they reward members in proportion to their contributions to joint ventures.

But fairness is only one sort of good among many and does not automatically take precedence over all others (contrary to the many writers on morality who place moral obligation above every other spring to action). When being fair is likely to lead to the frustration of all or most other important goals, rationality may dictate embarking on some other course of action. In the social arena, just as any other, the desire for fairness must be weighed in each case against the strengths of other, competing desires and sometimes must give ground. Victory in war, for example, frequently requires that burdens rest more heavily, and thus unfairly, on some compared to others. Being part of a primary in-group, a true society, entails standing ready to sacrifice in this way; it requires being willing to act out of a sense of duty to the group.

For most of us, the sense of duty is not unbounded. At one point or another, conflicting desires will be stronger than those of group loyalty. Although moved by the tug of duty, other sentiments may turn us in other directions. Just how far a rational person should go along the sacrificial path—at what point maximization of one's interests does not require sacrifice for the benefit of the group—is a serious and quite difficult question that is bound to be answered differently by one person as compared to others because of individual variations in the strengths of the different sorts of tugs on action. In any case, when unnecessarily overburdened with unfair duties, loyalty to the group becomes strained, as it does whenever unfairnesses of any kind go beyond a certain point (a matter to be discussed further in chapter 12). It is clear, however, that a group whose members are not seriously motivated by a sense of social duty does not merit the label *society* or *nation*.

In recent years, several theorists have championed so-called minimal, or night-watchman, states whose governments would limit their activities to keeping order and defending against outside aggression. One commonly voiced objection to minimal states is that they would lose out when competing with more traditional, full-blown states, an objection that seems to this writer to have a good deal of merit. But a more telling objection is that night-watchman states would not constitute true societies. They would be fundamentally different from the primary in-groups in which human beings always have lived, *and need to live,* if they are to lead satisfying lives.

The chief argument in favor of minimalist states is the allegedly immoral nature of full-blown governments. By their very nature, it is argued (differently by different theorists), governments are bound to restrict behavior in immoral ways. However, when morality is viewed in terms of contractual fairness, it becomes irrelevant into which areas governments intrude. Broadly empowered governments may, at least in theory, enact laws that are just as fair as those enacted by governments with a more restricted mandate. What counts is not the nature or topic of a law, but the procedure by which it is enacted and the way in which it treats a given citizen as compared to others. Night-watchman advocates often base their contrary view on the idea that governments in general tend to be unfair, so that "That government is best which governs least." But on the view being argued for here, the fundamental, underlying problem is the nature of human nature, not that of one sort of organization compared to others. (Obviously, more needs to be said on this matter, and it will be, in particular in chapters 10, 11, 13, and 21.)

10

Desirable Unfair Outcomes

Two wrongs *do* make a right, when the second compensates for the first.

—Harry Gardener

As remarked in the previous chapter, fairness is not the only factor a sensible electorate needs to take into account when deciding between competing courses of action. Economic considerations sometimes require unfair distributions of wealth, emergencies occasionally require greater sacrifices from some than others, and widespread feelings of compassion may dictate taking from Peter to aid Paul. Practices of this kind may be seen by a fair-minded electorate as desirable in spite of the fact that they unfairly benefit some members of the group at the expense of others.

Typically, measures of this kind at least indirectly benefit virtually everyone, although some gain a good deal more than others and some pay a larger price. Welfare measures that redistribute wealth from richer to poorer by means of progressive taxes are an example. Virtually everyone gains some benefits (increased security, greater civility, more pleasant surroundings, and so on), but obviously the poor gain more than the rich. Similarly, controlling interest rates and regulating the supply of money, when done intelligently, benefit virtually everyone by improving business conditions, but clearly costs and benefits tend to be unevenly distributed (as they are, for example, when lower interest rates benefit bondholders and higher rates harm those in the construction industry).

The friendlier a society, the larger the range of unfair practices that will be perceived as sufficiently desirable to warrant enactment. Misanthropic citizens, for example, are unlikely to see sufficient benefit from certain kinds of welfare measures, given that one motive urging their enactment is compassion.

One of the principal arguments against a more-than-minimal state is that redistributive taxes, because they take wealth from some and give it to others, are inherently unfair and therefore cannot rightly be enacted. (This is perhaps Robert Nozick's primary objection to larger kinds of states.) We have already pointed out a serious flaw in this way of looking at the matter: legislation unfair in itself may be fair in a meta sense if enacted by fair procedures. But this minimalist claim also can be rebutted by arguing that redistributive taxes can be regarded as measures that in part rectify the unfair advantages some (the rich and well-placed) have over others in capitalistic economies. (More is said on this point in chapter 21.)

Of course, a completely rational and fair-minded electorate would not adopt an unfair procedure when there is a fairer one readily available that would accomplish the same purpose. When television came on the scene earlier in this century, it was quickly realized by most people (other than anarchists and minimal-state theorists) that some sort of regulation was required. The choice made in the United States was to limit the number of channels in each area and then, in effect, to give them away to various "qualifying" parties. That some received these valuable gifts while others did not gave those so benefited an unfair competitive marketplace advantage. However, there were at least two equally practical and a good deal fairer alternatives: to auction off the available channels, or to make a sufficient number of channels available so that everyone able and willing to operate one could do so. Given these fairer alternatives, a rational and fair-minded electorate would not have chosen the unfair system actually adopted.

In addition to not choosing an unfair procedure when a fairer one is available, a rational and fair-minded electorate might well choose to adopt metaprocedures for handling alleged cases of unnecessary legal unfairness. They might, for instance, adopt a court procedure in which aggrieved parties could present arguments intended to show that a particular piece of legislation is patently both unfair *and* unnecessary, with success in such a plea forcing legislative reassessment.

In any case, when practicality does require unfair legislation, there are several ways in which the unfairness can be offset so as to render a whole social system less unfair over the long run, ways a genuinely fair-minded electorate would want to legislate. One would be to distribute unfair harms and benefits randomly, perhaps by means of a lottery. (This could be said to make a system meta-fair.) Another would be by rotating harms and benefits, or by requiring everyone to perform some sort of social service at a given age. Still another would be simply by providing offsetting benefits, so that, for example, soldiers who risk their lives in battle would be granted special opportunities, honor, and so on.

The point is that a society intent on maximizing fairness, but unwilling to unduly sacrifice practicality, can choose institutions and laws that disperse necessary harms and advantages as equally as possible over the long run so that in-group competition remains as fair as it can be made to be without seriously endangering the general welfare.

As might be expected, levying taxes that are in themselves unfair is one of the more practical ways to redress grievances resulting from otherwise desirable legislation. In particular, economic unfairness that is too costly to rectify directly can be compensated for in this way. In a capitalistic system, although there are great advantages to be gained by letting the marketplace decide wages (and prices), free markets tend to distribute the profits of common ventures unfairly. Those with great economic power can and generally do take advantage of those at the bottom of the economic ladder. Negative and progressive income taxes can right some of these wrongs.

It is true, of course, that some measures of this kind have undesirable side effects that need to be considered. The examples just mentioned have the unfortunate effect of reducing incentive. The higher a negative tax and the greater the progressivity of other taxes, the greater the likely loss in incentive. The point is that by enlightened manipulations of this kind, some measure of justice can be obtained without undue sacrifice of other society-wide benefits. How far a fair-minded electorate would be willing to go in the sacrifice of these other benefits depends on the extent of their desire for economic fairness.

There is at least one extremely important sort of case in which a sensible and fair-minded electorate might want to institute unfair measures in order to prevent a more serious kind of unfairness. Parents typically want to improve the chances of their offspring in life's competitions, for mates, jobs, status, and so on, and often do so in ways that require the expenditure of wealth. (Indeed, this frequently is the chief motive driving people to pile up more wealth than they can use to satisfy their own direct needs.) And yet, this tends to unfairly provide offspring of the rich with much better chances than the children of the rest of us. One obvious way to reduce this unfair advantage is by instituting otherwise unfair (because, for one thing, not fees for services rendered) inheritance taxes and other restrictions on the passing of wealth from one generation to the next, so that each generation has to start pretty much from

economic scratch. (Another, of course, is to provide educational opportunities for the children of ordinary citizens comparable to those
available to the rich.)

Money, however, is not the only or perhaps even the principal benefit parents disproportionately provide their offspring. Some parents nurture and motivate their children better than do others. The only way to
remedy the resulting unfairness, if it is genuinely unfair, is to require
that all children be raised in the same way, which means removing them
from the bosom of the family. But very few parents are likely to value
the fairness inherent in absolutely equal opportunity sufficiently to opt
for a society in which this kind of practice is the norm. Sentiments associated with kin altruism are stronger in most of us than are the reciprocal variety.

11

Civil Rights

That government is best which governs least.

—Variously attributed

Get off my back.

—Common saying

No ethical subjectivist can hold that there are natural or objective rights or liberties of any kind. On the contractual theory being espoused here, rights are generated in the same way as are obligations—by fair agreements. *Civil* rights are generated by society-wide agreements that require all citizens to relate to others in the group in certain ways. My right to free speech so generated thus creates your obligation to refrain from interfering with that liberty.

It follows, then, that there are no specific civil liberties that an electorate must institute to produce a fair society. Which rights sensible citizens will choose depends on how they perceive three factors: the likelihood that what is protected by a right otherwise might be infringed, how valuable its protection is perceived to be, and the practicality of its protection. Contracts guaranteeing freedom of religion, for example, are not needed in a society of atheists (nor, for that matter, in a religiously cohesive culture). Complete freedom of speech may be perceived as impractical (too expensive) by the members of a group constantly embroiled in clandestine machinations with a serious enemy. A right to privacy may lack any value whatever to members of an extremely cohesive, open, and sharing culture.

In fact, however, there are no completely atheistic societies and few, if any, that have complete religious cohesion. Freedom of speech has great practical value almost everywhere. And people in all large cul-

49

tures place a very high value on several different sorts of privacy. This may well be the principal reason that civil rights guaranteeing freedom of religion, speech, and so on, seem to be natural, or objective (another reason is discussed below), but it also constitutes good reason for supposing that a sensible electorate would opt for fair agreements instituting these sorts of rights in most cases.

The most commonly accepted civil right, no doubt, is the right to life, generally forfeitable only for extremely serious infractions of society-wide rules. (Indeed, in some cultures it is not forfeited under any circumstances.) On the view being championed here, a right to life is generated in the same way as any other civil right, namely by society-wide agreements that spell out the circumstances, if any, under which that right is to be protected or forfeited. Killing becomes *murder* only when proscribed by society-wide rules (or personal agreements).

Nevertheless, the feeling is widespread that a right to life is the most fundamental of all rights, to be dispensed with under no circumstances (although it can, perhaps, be forfeited). This feeling is so strong in most of us that it tends to persist in spite of the fact that almost all societies require the sacrifice of (innocent) life under certain circumstances ("in the line of duty," for example). From the contractual point of view, this feeling can be explained by the fact that it virtually always is in everyone's interest to be free from the gratuitous threat of death inflicted by others. (Note, of course, that capital punishment is not automatically ruled out by a contractual theory of moral obligation.)

Talk of a right to life brings to the fore the ongoing disputes concerning abortion. Those who argue that abortion is morally wrong generally do so on the grounds that a fetus is a living, innocent human being and that taking the life of an innocent human being is morally wrong (constitutes murder). But even supposing that a fetus is a living and innocent human being, it doesn't follow from the contractual point of view that fetuses have a right to life. The reason is that being human does not automatically entitle a person to the rights and privileges of a society. Whether a person has those rights depends on what sorts of agreements the citizens of that society have reached. A fetus is incapable of entering into agreements, which means that any rights it may have must flow from agreements made by the full-fledged citizens of the society into which it is born.[1]

---

[1]Interestingly, at most times and places throughout history, practical considerations have led people to "thin the rows" in one way or another, so as to avoid famine and widespread starvation, which, by the way, might abrogate a right to life of those who starve.

Similar remarks, incidentally, apply to newborn babies. Being incapable of entering into agreements of any kind, they have no rights not granted to them by society-wide agreements.[2]

Before leaving the topic of rights, the alleged natural right to engage in any sorts of behavior that do not significantly affect others needs to be considered. Getting drunk in the privacy of one's own home seems to be a different kind of activity, and more appropriately a *right*, than doing so in public. (Of course, getting drunk in private and then driving in public is another matter.) Why is this so?

Consider, as a typical example, a law forbidding cigarette smoking in the privacy of one's own home. To be fair, an agreement requiring smokers to sacrifice in this way must provide them some offsetting return. Yet in this case, there is no practical quid pro quo. (It would be impractical simply to pay smokers for not smoking in private, because then everyone would claim to be a frustrated smoker. Nor is it likely that those who oppose private smoking would be willing to prescribe this sort of restitution.) So enactment of a law against private smoking would be unfair to those who wish to light up in private. In addition, those harmed in this way would lack the usual motive rational and fair-minded citizens have for obeying a fairly enacted law that happens to harm them more than it does others, for their sacrifice would produce no society-wide benefit. Indeed, smokers would have good reason to flout the law,[3] which from their point of view would constitute unjustified punishment (because it would be inflicted in the absence of commission of an act having any harmful social effects).

---

[2]The same sort of reasoning obviously applies to disputes concerning alleged animal rights, with the exception that it may be, as some people including this writer believe, that some nonhuman animals (dogs, chimpanzees) are capable of entering into rudimentary agreements that, from the point of view being argued here, are as binding as any others.

[3]This point will be discussed further in the next chapter. But note here how enforcement of laws of this kind might easily be seen by those affected as unfairly reducing their competitive chances.

12

Rational Behavior in a Less-Than-Perfect World

Every actual state is corrupt. Good men must not obey the laws too well.

—Ralph Waldo Emerson

Is it not possible that an individual may be right and the government wrong? Are laws to be enforced simply because they are made? Or declared by any number of men to be good if they are not good?

—Henry David Thoreau

It's clear that in the case of a typical two-party agreement, failure of one party to comply releases the other from the obligation to do so. Being fair minded doesn't mean having to allow oneself to be played for a sucker. Nor is there reason in most cases in everyday life to deal further with those who have burned us in the past. If Smith has failed us in this way, there usually is some Jones we can turn to.

Similarly, being dealt with unfairly by organizations like sports, chess, or social clubs tends to release members from any moral (as opposed to legal) obligation to live up to the duties of membership. If a tennis club consistently fails to provide court access guaranteed by its rules and regulations, members dealt with in this cavalier way are justified in refusing to pay dues otherwise owed. Nor is there reason to continue membership. There generally are other clubs to turn to, and sports clubs are not a necessity of life in any case.

In chapter 9, we pointed out that the rules of fair play are not different with respect to one's primary in-group than they are for other groups, but that an in-group, a society, nevertheless is different from other kinds of organizations in several fundamental ways. In particular, resigning from an in-group is fraught with difficulties, penalties, and regrets not encountered when withdrawing from a chess club or mutual fund.

The full import of this difference is obvious in the case of an extremely oppressive society, or one in which certain groups are not granted first-class citizenship. Slaves on a Southern plantation in 1820, for example, not being able to emigrate or revolt, had no alternative to knuckling under and protecting themselves against tyranny and oppression in whatever ways came to hand. The point is that they certainly had no moral obligation to be scrupulous about obeying the laws and customs of a society that systematically treated them so unfairly.

But what about citizens of less tyrannical societies, burdened only by the usual kinds of unfair dealings that have plagued human social intercourse throughout history? In general, a principle of proportionality is relevant in their case: the greater the unfairness their society subjects them to, the less obligated they are to scrupulously adhere to its rules and regulations.

There are several interesting sorts of cases to which this principle of proportionality is relevant. One concerns obedience to particular rules or customs that are widely flouted. Those who cheat, say, on income tax laws (as most do in virtually every large society), gain a competitive advantage on those who are scrupulously honest. Clearly, then, just as in the case of a two-person agreement where one party's failure tends to release the other from contractual obligations, so also with respect to society-wide agreements, the noncompliance of large numbers of citizens in a society tends to absolve others of their obligations to comply. Being moral doesn't entail being a patsy.

Of course, that some cheat on their income tax obligations in small ways does not justify others doing so in a wholesale manner. That a few cheat constitutes less of an excuse for disobedience than if many are guilty. Similarly, that a few laws are flouted in this way provides less justification for noncompliance than if laws in general tend to be disregarded.

Tax laws also are relevant to another interesting kind of case, because they nicely illustrate problems related to the bribery and corruption that provide those who are rich and powerful with unfair advantages in the lawmaking process.[1] Small operators of "ma and pa" retail stores, for in-

---

[1]Recall, however, what was said before about the external "talent" of money and about what games we wish to play. Most of us prefer to play the game of politics construed so that ability to bribe is not a relevant talent; we tend to see the game of politics as unfair when the ability to corrupt is frequently the winning talent. But the hard-nosed among us may see things differently.

stance, lack the clout of big oil producers and dairy firms; they can't bribe legislatures into passing special measures setting minimum prices or granting depletion allowances. But they can keep two sets of books, one accurate and the other for tax purposes, as a way of evening the score. Again, of course, the more widespread the corruption of the legislative process happens to be, the greater the justification in a particular case for defensive cheating on the part of those who lack corrupting clout.

A similar kind of case arises with respect to disproportionate enforcement of otherwise fair laws. Take municipal real estate tax laws assessed at a specified percentage of the value of property. In many, perhaps most, United States cities and towns, real estate owned by many rich or politically connected citizens tends to be seriously undervalued. Ordinary homeowners who fail to take advantage of the more modest sorts of opportunities available to them, say by neglecting to report improvements that increase the value of their holdings, miss opportunities to make the playing field a bit closer to level. The point, of course, is that governmental failure to equitably enforce an otherwise fair law tends to absolve those thereby harmed of the obligation to scrupulously comply.

Modestly different thoughts apply to the question of obedience to laws or customs proscribing behavior that is not harmful to others, say viewing pornographic movies or smoking marijuana in the privacy of one's own castle.[2] As noted in the previous chapter, those whose behavior is restricted by these laws have little incentive to obey them when there is no significant social benefit gained by doing so. In addition, noncompliance sometimes is justified by knowledge that the elected officials who voted for these measures did so merely to gain political advantage (championing a "war" against drug use, for instance, has often been a potent political ploy). That most of the citizens who favored passage of these bills have been misled by authority figures using demagogic or other propagandistic techniques tends to sour respect for this sort of legislation among those who understand what has happened, just as when out-and-out intimidation or coercion is known to have been employed.

Similar remarks apply to legislation that for political reasons is poorly

---

[2]There are, of course, those who argue that these activities do indeed have adverse public effects. Looking at pornographic films, for example, has often been claimed to increase the likelihood of overt sexual crimes. But even supposing this is true (and the evidence in the case of pornography seems meager at best), the points made in the previous chapter against proscribing private behavior would apply, unless, perhaps, it could be shown that looking at pornography in the privacy of one's own home always leads to the commission of sexual crimes.

focused, so that a genuine evil is addressed at the expense of many or to the benefit of a few. The 1920's prohibition of the consumption of alcoholic beverages in the United States, the "great experiment," is a good example, since it targeted millions of alcohol enthusiasts, whose conduct while under the influence harmed no one else, along with the much smaller number of those who drank and drove or who failed to fulfill obligations to others because they had become alcoholics.

The point is that after weighing the strengths of the relevant countervailing forces and considering each case on its merits, citizens who are on the whole fair minded may sometimes conclude quite correctly that they are not bound, or only partially bound, by certain society-wide agreements.[3]

No doubt there are many who will find the idea that it is sometimes rational, and not unfair, to violate fairly enacted laws quite shocking. But consider some other examples of essentially private activities that have at one time or place been made illegal.

Until quite recently, several states in the United States proscribed all kinds of nonmarital sexual intercourse, whether of the hetero or homo variety, and prohibited a great many perfectly ordinary kinds of sexual behavior even when engaged in by married couples in the privacy of their own bedrooms. For the unmarried, scrupulous obedience to such laws meant complete abstention (of lifetime duration in the case of homosexuals and of heterosexuals who never marry) from this extremely compelling and human activity. For a great many married couples, it entailed abstention from various ways in which they commonly carry on this activity. Small wonder that upstanding citizens have generally chosen to ignore these restrictions on their sexual behavior.

Those still shocked might consider the countless cases of intolerant laws concerning the practice of religion that have peppered the history of the human species. Think, just for starters, of regulations that have made it illegal to practice any but a preferred religion (sometimes on pain of death), and then only in some orthodox manner, or that have re-

---

[3]It generally is foolish to enact relatively unenforceable measures, even if obedience to those measures would bring about desirable consequences, a point illustrated nicely by the repeated failure of anti-drug and anti-pornography laws. Legal laws do not rescind the laws of human nature. (Note also the connection to the topic of civil rights discussed in the previous chapter. A sensible electorate will take account of the extreme difficulty, if not impossibility, of enforcing certain kinds of behavior, and one way they can do so is by enacting civil rights legislation guaranteeing the legitimacy of primarily private activities.)

quired acceptance of a favored religious doctrine. Or consider the many times when all those who honestly professed to the "wrong" religious beliefs, or to none at all, have been barred from most positions of any consequence. (Nor have all of these odious religious laws been enacted by undemocratic means or against the will of the people.) Small wonder that fair-minded citizens have so often resorted to lying through their teeth by professing falsely to religious doctrines, while countless others have been forced to practice their religions clandestinely.

While some cases in which a fair-minded person might justifiably violate a fairly enacted law are clear-cut, most are not. Whether or not to comply with a given piece of legislation often comes down to a matter of degree. How frequently is the law flouted? How fairly is it enforced? How oppressive is it perceived to be? How fair were the procedures under which it was enacted? In everyday life, clear-cut answers to these questions tend to be hard to come by.

Mention of procedural fairness brings to the fore the practical point that we can't demand perfect procedural fairness before feeling bound to comply with offensive regulations. There have never been and are unlikely ever to be any but the tiniest societies in which complete procedural fairness is even approximated. The United States, for instance, stands reasonably high on the procedural fairness scale, and yet several modestly serious flaws are built into its procedural system. Recall that a decision procedure is fair only if those affected have an equal voice, a requirement that in a system of representative government is satisfied only if the vote of each elected member of a legislative body reflects size of constituency. In the United States, this requirement comes modestly close to being met in the House of Representatives, but is very far from being satisfied in the Senate, where, for instance, the two senators from Alaska are the voice of about 400,000 citizens while the two from California represent over 30 million. The point here is that we can't use the existence of this kind of procedural unfairness as a blanket excuse for violating whatever laws or customs we perceive as unfair or otherwise odious.

Finally, it's interesting that the kind of noncompliance with law most frequently discussed by philosophers in the past thirty years or so has been not any of the cases discussed above but rather the very special and unusual case of "civil disobedience" (a technical term). Roughly speaking, as used by philosophers, the term applies to unlawful actions performed in protest of a particular law or laws, usually including violation of the offending law or laws, where the protestors make no attempt to avoid prosecution and are, on the contrary, willing to suffer punishment in the cause of justice as they perceive it. The goal of those who engage in civil disobedience is not to gain personal benefit from clandestinely disobeying an odious law, as, say, in the case of those who take illegal drugs for their own pleasure. It is, rather, to work for the repeal of an offending statute or custom by moving society to perceive its unfair nature. Civil disobedience thus has a much higher tone about it ᵗhan disobedience prompted by the desire to satisfy personal interests.

13

Capitalism versus Socialism

> If the world is lucky enough to enjoy peace, it may even one day
> make the discovery, to the horror of doctrinaire free-enterprisers
> and doctrinaire planners alike, that what is called capitalism and
> what is called socialism are both capable of working quite well.
> —John Kenneth Galbraith

Just as the issue between minimal and more full-blown governments
cannot be decided by appeals to fairness, so also we can't settle disputes
between advocates of socialism and of capitalism in this way. Even supposing that capitalism, having competition at its very core, is a less
friendly economic system than socialism (a common claim to be considered soon), it doesn't follow that it is an inherently unfair system. As
argued in chapter 6, fairness in itself is not inconsistent with a good deal
of unfriendly competition.

Economists, of course, have argued endlessly about the virtues and
defects of capitalism and socialism. Some argue for a pure system of one
kind or the other; most contend that a felicitous blend of the two would
produce the greatest overall economic benefits for a society as a whole.
But most of their disputes concern issues properly fought over in the political arena on grounds of practicality (and perhaps taste) as well as fair
play; they cannot be resolved by appeals to principles of fair play alone.

There are, however, two alleged advantages of socialism over capitalism to which questions of fairness seem to be particularly relevant.
One is that, unlike socialism, capitalism by its very nature rigs the competitive deck in favor of some citizens and against others. Fairness requires that the games sanctioned by a society be fair to all participants
and, therefore, that everyone have an equal opportunity for success.
Capitalism, it is claimed, much more than socialism, must fail in this re-

spect. The rich, proponents of this view argue, inevitably gain immense political power, which they can, and frequently do, use to slant the playing field in their favor. On a more personal level, when competing for jobs and acquiring personal wealth, the rich have available the advantages of nepotism, cronyism, and a superior education. Under a socialistic economic system, the argument goes, these advantages of great wealth disappear so that, in general, the playing field is closer to level.

There are two reasons for doubting the cogency of this argument. The first is that the advantages gained by wealth in a capitalistic system can be reduced considerably by various means available to an informed and intelligent electorate, including the enactment of stiff inheritance taxes, legislation forbidding nepotism and cronyism, and the universal availability of high quality public schools.[1] The second is that socialistic systems provide just as many opportunities for stacking the deck as do those that are capitalistic. Individuals wielding political power are just as likely to use it for personal or familial advantage as are those whose power is economic. The culprit is not a particular economic system but rather the competitive nature of the human animal. We cannot change that competitive nature by opting for one economic system rather than another. To increase the fairness of whatever economic system we may choose on other grounds (for instance, for the sake of productivity) requires the eternal vigilance that is the well-known price of liberty, coupled with an informed and intelligent electorate. In any case, a *completely* fair society is improbable because of the unlikelihood that we shall ever see an eternally vigilant citizenry, not to mention one that is sufficiently informed and intelligent.

The other commonly alleged advantage of socialism over capitalism that is relevant here is that capitalism, much more than socialism, tends to make people much less fair-minded. It does so, it is claimed, because, unlike socialism, competition is at its roots. The point of this argument is that competitive activities tend to make selfish interests dominate those counseling fair play. But this claim is suspect also. For one thing, as just remarked, competition is built into the very nature of the human condition; it does not arise from the institution of this system or that but from the fact that we are each other's most serious competitors for the goods

---

[1]Measures of this kind often are thought to be socialistic in nature, one reason some theorists argue for mixed socialistic/capitalistic systems. But they aren't necessarily socialistic if by that concept one has in mind common ownership of the basic means of production.

that make life worthwhile. For another, competitive instincts and our sense of fair play are not entirely antithetical; witness the strong desire most of us have to compete fairly and the greater satisfaction we derive from winning fair and square as compared to when we cheat. And for still another, the claim that capitalistic systems tend more than their socialistic counterparts to bring out the more aggresssive, less fair-minded, side of the human repertoire is unproved and indeed unlikely. Every system, no matter what its economic base, must find ways to distribute the material goods, services, honors, and power that human beings seek. So there will be severe competition to obtain these assets no matter what sort of system is used to determine their production and distribution.

On the other side of the ledger, it sometimes is claimed that a socialistic system is bound to be less fair in practice than a capitalistic one because of the way power is distributed in these two kinds of systems. Under a democratic capitalistic system, political and economic power, theoretically, are separate, although, of course, economic power tends to generate political power. But under socialism, it is said, political and economic power are, by the nature of the system, in the same few hands. If it is true that when fewer hold power the likelihood of tyranny is greater, it follows that the few who have both economic and political power under socialism are more likely to run roughshod over the masses than are larger numbers of capitalists who wield only economic power.

The trouble with this theory is not that concentrated power is more likely to produce tyranny than power that is diffuse. It is, rather, first, that in democratic societies, whether of the socialistic or capitalistic variety, governmental power is not concentrated in the hands of a few. Bureaucrats wield a good deal of it (as United States presidents who come and go quickly discover to their dismay), and elected officials who control the legislative process are not necessarily of one mind. Further, that power under any democratic system tends either to be captured by a few or not depends, as mentioned before, on the vigilance, intelligence, etc., of the people governed. (Note that in the real world today, well-placed individuals and organizations in both capitalistic and in socialistic societies have in fact captured an inordinate amount of political and economic power.)[2]

---

[2]It seems likely, in any case, that modern industrial-scientific societies are reaching a level of complexity at which attempts by a very few to control all economic or political activity more and more are going to fail. This does not mean, however, that all kinds of socialistic systems are bound to fail! It does mean, however, that those in which an oligarchy directs matters from the top down, without significant input from those governed, are very likely to do so.

In any case, competition in modern societies tends to be less and less over the the raw physical necessities of life (food, clothing, and shelter) and more and more over the positional goods (including fame, honor, and fashionable items) that signify status—goods that by their nature can never be manufactured so as to satisfy demand. Who owns or controls the production of goods that in theory can be indefinitely reproduced thus becomes less and less important; increasingly it is the control of status items that matters. The advent in the twenty-first century of virtually unlimited and extremely cheap power (obtained by nuclear fusion, photosynthesis, etc.) will almost certainly make these positional goods the central items fought over in future competitive arenas.

14

Fair Taxes

Taxation without representation is tyranny.

—James Otis

The subjects of every state ought to contribute towards the support of government as nearly as possible in proportion to their respective abilities; that is, in proportion to the revenue which they respectively enjoy under the protection of the state.

—Adam Smith

To be completely fair, a tax law, like any law, has to be fair to every citizen. This means that fair taxes have to be commensurate with benefits received and thus be *fair fees for services or products rendered*. A law that takes more from a citizen in taxes than is returned in benefits cannot in itself be fair to that person (although, as remarked before, it can be instituted in order to counteract other sorts of unfair measures). Note, however, that fair play may, and often does, require adherence to unfair tax laws enacted by fair procedures. The fairness of the procedure, the fact that there is taxation *with* representation, renders unfair tax measures so instituted fair in a broader sense. (But recall the remarks in chapter 12 concerning the rationality of adherence to unfair laws.)

When all taxpayers gain equal value from a particular service, or there is no practical way to calculate even approximate differences, the fair price for that service to a given taxpayer, and thus the fair tax, has to be 1/Nth of the total costs to society (where N = the number of taxpayers).

Of course, few, if any, services are of equal value to everyone. Public highways, for example, are more valuable to those with private automobiles than to others, even though they provide some benefit to everyone. And even protection from outside aggressors may be of greater value to some than to others: the very rich or the politically powerful may stand to lose more by defeat and to gain more by victory than the average citizen. Completely fair taxes must reflect these differences in benefits, as gasoline taxes do when they are used to pay for highway maintenance, and as property taxes based on assessed valuations do when used to pay part of the costs of fire and police protection.

The same sort of reasoning applies even to an institution such as a public school system. Everyone benefits from the education of all young people in a society, and so fairness requires that every taxpayer pay part of the costs of public schools. But the parents of schoolchildren benefit a great deal more than do other taxpayers. Fairness thus requires that these parents pay a larger share of the costs than other taxpayers. (Note, however, that fairness does not require that there be an institution such as a public school system. It requires only that if there is such an institution, its costs should be fairly divided.) Of course, there may well be reasons for preferring an unfair tax system that does not dun poor parents for the total cost of educating their children (the benefits accruing to everyone in society when all children are well-educated immediately spring to mind, as does the thought that providing free education to the poor might be a good way to rectify any unfairnesses those at the bottom of the economic heap might be subject to). But that is another matter.

Although the general way in which fair taxes are to be calculated is reasonably clear, determining exact numbers tends to be rather difficult. Take taxes levied to support public school education. As we have just observed, fairness requires that the parents of schoolchildren bear a greater share of the supporting tax burden, but exactly how much greater should their tax burden be? The theoretical answer is that it depends on the value of a public school education. Yet it is notoriously difficult, even in contrived theoretical cases, to determine the value of a commodity of this sort. This doesn't mean that approximations are impossible or that there is no point in trying to come to as fair a judgment as we can. It means simply that questions concerning fair taxes cannot be answered merely by appeals to set principles; they need to be hashed out in the political arena, where intuitions concerning fairness and value, at least in the minds of a fair-minded electorate, set approximate limits.

So far, we have considered the fairness of taxes levied as fees for services rendered. But taxes may be fair when enacted for other purposes, including to finance socialistic economic measures. The British investment in North Sea oil provides an example. Measures of this kind are fair if they return profits (and losses) in proportion to the amount of taxes assessed, again on the principle that those who pay more should receive proportionately more. (The reason funds raised to finance such ventures constitute taxes is that they are involuntary from the point of view of individual "investors" even though everyone has a voice in their adoption.)

As remarked before, taxes also can be used to redistribute wealth. Because the rich have much greater political power than do ordinary citizens, the poor in particular, this redistribution usually is from less affluent taxpayers to the more affluent much more than the other way around. The rich are benefited more in this way when industries are given government subsidies (agribusiness, the oil industry); when "pork" legislation for unneeded or marginal programs is passed by legislatures; when publicly owned wealth is given to private parties (the airwaves) or sold to them for well below market value (mineral rich land, grazing and water rights); when taxes on wealthy individuals are set at a level below what fairness (in the sense of fees for services) would require; when industries are protected by import and other taxes that discourage foreign competition; and so on. But ordinary citizens and the poor also are benefited by redistributive measures, for example, by welfare redistributions to poor mothers who have dependent children and by measures designed to benefit those who are physically or mentally handicapped.

It can be argued that most of the redistributions to the poor, in particular to the working poor, can be seen as fair in that they tend to offset other sorts of unfairnesses that may be desirable for other reasons (as discussed before and again in the next chapter). But most of the tax unfairnesses that benefit the rich, and very few of those benefiting the poor, cannot be justified in this way.

Some tax unfairnesses, however, may be justified on other grounds. It has been argued, for example, that industry subsidies are good for the overall economy and thus are justified on practical grounds, and that taxes used to benefit the handicapped or the non-working poor are desirable on grounds of compassion and indirect benefits to other citizens or to the economy as a whole.

15

Fair Play in the Marketplace

Caveat emptor.
—Legal maxim

The market is the place apart where men may deceive each other.
—Anacharsis (quoted by Diogenes Laertius)

How many men are there who fairly earn a million dollars?
—Henry George (and many others)

We should expect intuitions concerning fair play in the marketplace to be much less precise, less complete, and perhaps even less consistent than those concerning most other areas of human endeavor. Human beings have been designed by evolutionary forces to thrive in quite different, simpler circumstances, unlike those encountered in today's economic arenas. Nevertheless, we are not completely devoid of sentiments concerning economic fair play.

Interactions in the economic world are of three basic varieties: exclusively competitive (competing retailers who happen never to cooperate); chiefly competitive but partly cooperative (traders on commodities exchanges); and chiefly cooperative but partly competitive (workers in a large corporation).[1] Of course, there are no sharp lines between these three types. The workers, management, and stockholders of a large corporation may engage in more, or less, hard-nosed bargaining for the profits of their common endeavors; competing retailers may, or may not, conspire to set prices.

---

[1]There also are unusual cases in which economic activities are carried out almost exclusively on a cooperative basis—nonprofit organizations (and kibbutzim?) perhaps being examples.

While competing economic organizations may indeed cooperate with each other, and frequently do, the nature of their relationships in the marketplace does not require cooperation. But the buying and selling of goods, by its very nature, requires at least a modicum of cooperation (each trader depends on the others to come through with the agreed-upon goods); and being part of a large corporation requires a good deal more.

Well, then, what sort of market *system,* as opposed to individual market games, would a sensible electorate choose? Clearly, the one that they believe most likely to maximize long-term benefits for society as a whole. So if experience indicates that a modestly unfair, or somewhat unfriendly, market economy produces more or higher quality goods than does one that is completely fair, or extremely friendly, sensible citizens will take that fact into account when deciding which system to adopt. This doesn't mean automatically opting for the most productive system. Fair-minded citizens, for example, may well prefer a less efficient but fairer or friendlier system to one that maximizes productivity. They might even choose to reduce both efficiency and fairness in order to more effectively aid the downtrodden.

As a matter of fact, however, no industrial society has ever opted for a completely friendly economic system. At one time or another, they all have permitted players to conduct their activities in unfriendly ways, either by taking advantage of the ignorance, foolishness, stupidity, misfortune, or economic distress of other players, or by failing to fulfill contractual obligations, or by effectively freezing some players out of the market for particular commodities. It's not surprising, of course, that no free markets have ever made all kinds of advantage takings illegal. Doing so would mean, for instance, forbidding players from taking advantage of the economic weaknesses of others by driving down the prices of goods in oversupply or by jacking up the prices of items in great demand, either of which proscriptions would go a long way towards rescinding the law of supply and demand on which the success of a free market depends.

In any case, an economic system designed to permit most kinds of advantage takings still could be competitively fair (although it obviously would be rather hard-nosed). The point is academic, of course, given that there has never been a genuinely competitively fair marketplace of any size or sophistication, nor is there likely to be. Most markets permit a certain amount of restraint of trade, thus being unfair to those conspired against, and all in fact grant greater opportunities to certain favored competitors than to the run of the herd.

But no industrial society has ever allowed every sort of unfriendly economic competition. There are, after all, obvious advantages in opening a market to all comers,[2] in enacting laws that enforce legitimate contracts, in having statutes that forbid misrepresentation or the secret use of insider information, and so on. The trick is to find the mix of friendly and unfriendly competitive activities that maximizes the benefits a well-run economic system can produce.

Turning to questions concerning cooperative fairness, note first that easy answers are forthcoming only in the relatively few cases in which the contributions of the various parties to a common venture are easily compared, as they are, for example, when one partner contributes twice as much effort, knowledge, or capital as another. Nevertheless, we do have a few sentiments, admittedly vague, to guide us in more difficult cases.

Consider the values of various kinds of labor. Some theorists (Marxists?) believe that an hour of labor of one kind is equal in value to an hour of any other and thus should be equally rewarded. But this sentiment is not widely shared. Most of us tend to see more *effective* or *important* labor, other things being equal, as meriting a greater slice of profits than labor that is less productive, or relatively trivial. We also tend to see labor that is more odious, tedious, or unhealthy, or that requires greater skill, as meriting greater rewards. (Note, by the way, that in the real world, odious, tedious, and unhealthy jobs, the ones that are the least desirable, tend to be among the lowest paying.)

An obvious difficulty with our intuitions about these important matters is that they are comparative, not quantitative. But there are other problems with them as well. For one thing, judgments differ considerably as to which kinds of labor are more odious, or tedious. Daredevil types, for example, seek out risky, and thus thrilling, jobs most of us could not stand; some people find teaching, or the writing of books or articles, a good deal more tedious than do others. For another, judgments differ a good deal concerning the importance, or value, of the finished products of various kinds of labor. Classical music lovers value the labor of concert violinists a good deal more highly than do people with tin ears; the values of the effects of drugs such as alcohol, or of the services of prostitutes, differ notoriously from person to person. And for still another, it isn't always easy even to determine how particular

---

[2]Or perhaps only to all qualified comers, since it may be undesirable to allow all applicants into certain professions, such as medicine.

individuals value labor. Expressed judgments often reflect selfish interests rather than accurate evaluations.[3]

Nor is it absolutely clear that the way a given person values a particular kind of labor dovetails with that individual's sentiments concerning fair wages. There is a sense, for instance, in which most of us tend to value our own labor, however productive, in much the same way; it is, after all, equally precious in being the chief resource we have for obtaining life's necessities. Yet most would agree that the fair return for labor should be greater for the more productive than for those who produce less.[4]

How then can we compare, say, the efforts of waiters with those of chefs, the exertions of hairdressers with those of nurses, or the labor of computer programmers with those of computer designers? Assuming that fair wages for chief executive officers generally should be somewhat higher than for assembly line workers, how much higher should they be? (It is commonly held that most of the top executives of large American corporations, many of whom are paid more in one year than most assembly line workers earn in a lifetime, are grossly overpaid, but even if this intuition is on target, it doesn't provide us with an easy or automatic formula for determining what fair executive salaries would be like.)

In any case, we need to remember that subjectivists, when attempting to determine what constitutes a fair wage, cannot appeal to such things as *the* value, or the *objectively correct* value, of labor irrespective of particular human evaluations. That is why it is so theoretically important that different people (even when not being self-deceived) frequently evaluate labor differently, as do employers (buyers of labor), who tend to see labor value in terms of the end products it produces, while employees (sellers of labor) calculate more in terms of time and effort expended.

It often is argued that we can at least specify a "living wage," which then can serve as a lower limit on wages. That there are hardworking citizens in relatively prosperous societies who cannot afford proper health care, nourishing food, or anything remotely resembling decent housing

---

[3]It isn't just that people tend to lie out of self-interest, although that certainly happens often enough, but rather that, when personal interests are at stake, self-deception tends to skew judgment. One reason that moral theorists introduce devices such as "ideal observers" is precisely to reduce this kind of (usually) unconscious bias.

[4]The issue is clouded by the fact that commodities, including labor, tend to be evaluated differently depending on circumstances. Food, for example, is worth a great deal more to someone who is starving than to the well fed; those desperate for work are bound to value their labor quite differently from people who are independently wealthy.

often is taken as evidence that their wages are unfair. Anyone in a relatively prosperous society who performs full-time useful work, it is argued, merits at least a minimum standard of living. But how is this to be determined? What, for example, constitutes sufficiently adequate housing? And what reason is there for supposing that fair compensation for every kind of useful employment is indeed a living wage?[5]

Of course, in a completely free marketplace, wages are determined primarily by supply and demand. When labor is scarce, pay scales rise;[6] when it is in overly great abundance, they decline, sometimes to the point that those at the bottom of the economic heap cannot afford things such as decent housing, proper health care, or adequate amounts of nourishing food. That is one reason why so many theorists argue in favor of minimum wage laws, or for a negative income tax that compensates for the effects of free market forces; they find it unacceptable that anyone who does useful work should be unable to afford the necessities of modern life.

Indeed, most of us view this as unacceptable. But why? Is it because sentiments concerning cooperative fair play tell us that low-income workers deserve a larger slice of the economic pie than market forces provide or is it, perhaps, because of compassion?

One way to approach this question is to think about related intuitions concerning those who are unable to perform (sufficiently) useful work—those who are seriously handicapped, mentally defective, seriously ill, or injured. At first glance, it would seem that if the benefits of cooperative ventures are parceled out according to input, then these people cannot claim a living wage as their fair share of profits. Yet most of us find their neglect unacceptable, just as as we do the underpayment of the gainfully employed. That we feel this way points to compassion directed towards fellow citizens in distress, not to intuitions concerning

---

[5]It can be argued, for instance, that when employers find an employee's work, although useful at some price, not worth a specified minimum wage, then the fair wage for that person is below the specified minimum. (One of the horrendously difficult problems facing most industrial societies in the twenty-first century is that the value to potential employers of the labor of increasingly large numbers of people very likely will be less than what will be thought of as a living wage.)

[6]In the fourteenth century, when plague swept through western Europe, the wages of common laborers rose dramatically because workers were in short supply and thus could demand a larger share of the profits of common ventures than they could before calamity struck. (Every cloud has a silver lining.)

fairness, as the principal reason so many of us want those unable to work, and, by analogy, low-paid workers, to receive at least a minimum income. It points to our sense of community, to our regard for the welfare of fellow citizens, not to intuitions concerning fair play, as the reason we find the neglect of those in distress unacceptable.

On the other hand, the handicapped and workers at the bottom of the pay scale are citizens of their society, with the same rights generated by the social contract as the rest of us. Just as there is at least an implied social agreement in a well run society to come to the aid of those in distress (say, when natural disasters strike or someone is hit by an automobile), so also, it can be argued, citizens in dire need are covered by an insurance proviso that can be regarded as an implicit part of the social contract. Looked at in this way, the unacceptability of the suffering of fellow citizens receiving less than a living wage, or of those unable to work because of illness or accidental injury, can be thought of as reflecting the willingness, even the desire, of most citizens who identify strongly with their own in-group to enter into society-wide agreements requiring them to come to the aid of equally disposed fellow citizens in distress. Perhaps, then, help rendered by society to those in need can, after all, be regarded as their right under an implied in-group contract that is cooperatively fair (fair because the insured contribute equally by standing ready to aid others in distress, while at the same time equally sharing the benefit of having others standing ready to come to their aid).[7]

It also may be argued that fair play requires us to provide certain minimum benefits to those individuals who obey the laws and customs of their group, since we all receive a benefit from their compliance (witness the costs inflicted on us by those, in particular criminals, who fail to conform). We can't expect (or demand?) that individuals forced by market conditions to work hard for less than a living wage, or who are

---

[7]Note, however, that this line of reasoning works all the way through only with respect to those who, prior to their needing help, were able (and willing?) to come to the aid of others in distress. A social contract can be cooperatively fair only if potential recipients of aid also are potential providers. Otherwise, its benefits (insurance against serious difficulties) will not be distributed according to input (ability and willingness to provide aid). A fair social insurance contract thus can't cover those (in particular, the insane and genetically handicapped) who lack even the potential ability to properly take part. If these citizens are to be covered by society-wide insurance contracts, it must be via agreements entered into by others, which suggests that it must be compassion, or similar other-regarding sentiments, that underpin the feelings most of us have that the seriously handicapped should be helped.

willing to work but cannot find jobs, be scrupulous in obeying the laws of the land. (Nor is there good reason for them to be; hardship finally does, and often rationally ought to, overcome normal desires to play the game according to the rules.)

In any case, when trying to determine fair wages, in particular for high rollers, we need to remember that no person is an island. Whatever a given member of a society accomplishes is due in large part to the knowledge and opportunity provided by the group as a whole. The three inventors of the transistor, to take one example, produced an item of tremendous value, but in calculating their fair remuneration, we need to factor in the contributions of society, especially in the form of education, and, in this case, the contributions of their employer, the Bell Laboratories of AT&T. (Similar remarks apply to Robert Nozick's famous Wilt Chamberlain example; Chamberlain may well have deserved a larger share of profits than other players of his day, but not the huge amounts Nozick thinks justified. More will be said about this in chapter 21.)

We also need to notice that material goods, including money, are only one kind of payment for services. In the case of outstanding producers — the Mozarts, Newtons, Lincolns, and even Wilt Chamberlains of the world — fame, honor, power, and in extreme cases immortality, are perhaps the principal sorts of deserved remuneration. It makes sense to say, for example, that the inventors of the transistor were rewarded handsomely by being granted Nobel prizes, even though their monetary compensation was not great (as these things go). (Chamberlain achieved worldwide fame and, if he is to be believed, also was rewarded with access to virtually unlimited numbers of women.)

In the discussion of fair wages so far, we have been thinking of those engaged in cooperative ventures chiefly with respect to their roles as cooperators, neglecting the fact that they also are competitors (although this aspect of the matter certainly lurked in the background when the effects of supply and demand on wages, and of self-deception on our perceptions of fair wages, were mentioned). After all, salaries in free marketplaces tend to be determined not by considerations of cooperative fairness but rather by competitive infighting. Judgments about salary fairness tend to be colored by the fact that cooperators also are competitors.

In real-life marketplaces, the line between cooperative and competitive interactions is very fine, exactly how fine depending on the degree of friendliness of the competitive games that are permitted in a given economic system. This is true in particular with respect to transactions between buyers and sellers.

Consider, for example, a situation in which a publishing company has its own marketing division that sells its products to bookstores. Determining fair wages for members of its sales force thus becomes primarily a matter of calculating each individual's cooperatively fair share of overall corporate profits. Now suppose that the publisher abolishes its marketing division and signs contracts with its members, so that they now are independent contractors who buy books from the publisher and then sell them to bookstores at a price, specified by the publisher, which yields the now independent parties a good deal less income than they formerly were paid as their fair share of company profits. Having become separate agents, their commissions become a matter of contractual bargaining, a competitive activity in which cooperative fairness tends to recede into the background. (The contracts reached in this way are competitively fair provided only that the rules which society has set up for the buying and selling of goods are competitively fair and that the parties involved have adhered to them.)

But what is the difference between the two ways of selling books that should make such a large difference? In similar cases that have occurred recently in the United States, courts have sometimes held that the switch to independent contractors constitutes a subterfuge designed to circumvent payment of certain fringe benefits the law requires employers to provide (in particular, health and retirement benefits). It is as though courts have held that these allegedly independent contractors really are company employees in disguise and therefore deserve a cooperatively fair wage, not merely whatever their competitive positions in the marketplace permit them to gain as sellers of a service (their own labor) to a willing buyer.

Another way to look at the matter is to remember that degrees of competition between buyers and sellers differ with respect to the friendliness of their trading interactions. The friendlier such transactions are, the less the prices of goods they trade will be determined by competitive factors such as supply and demand (true friends, for instance, don't jack up prices in line with market forces) and the more they will be decided in accordance with principles of cooperative fair play. So we can see the shift from in-house sales representative to independent contractor as involving a deliberate diminution of friendliness forced on booksellers by the book publisher (note, for instance, that any loyalty due the corporation disappears when an employee is turned into an independent agent).

Attempts to determine fair returns on invested capital encounter problems similar to those concerning fair wages. For example, it generally is thought proper, and not just economically sensible, that money placed in a guaranteed bank account should receive a lower rate of return than funds invested in a risky start-up company. The principle involved here, as in the case of fair wages, is a qualitative one: as risk increases, fair portions of resulting profits should increase. But how do we measure *degree* of risk?

Discussion of ways to determine fair shares of the profits of cooperative ventures inevitably raises the further question of *fair prices* for goods produced. After all, the profits earned by most such ventures are determined in large part by the prices of the goods they make and then sell. (In this age of specialization, very few organizations produce goods that are to be consumed only, or even primarily, by their own members.) But, assuming there are such things as fair prices, how are they to be calculated?

The most plausible, or at least straightforward, way is simply to add up all of a venture's expenses, including a fair return on wages and invested capital. Fair prices for all of that enterprise's commodities then should equal these expenses. The trouble is that this method depends on there being an independent way to determine fair wages and fair returns on invested capital, both of which we have characterized in terms of share of venture profits. We can't then determine fair profits (which depend in large part on prices) by reference to fair wages and fair returns on capital. (There also, of course, is the problem of parceling out the share of expenses to assign to each of an enterprise's different products.)

The trouble here is generated in part by our failure to first specify what sort of fairness we have in mind when we speak of *fair* prices. To be competitively fair, prices merely have to be agreed to by traders obeying whatever competitive rules (assuming they are fair) govern the economic games in question. To be cooperatively fair, trading prices have to divide the profits of trades according to the input of each trader. The problem, of course, is to find a way to calculate input.

One way that is at least of theoretical interest is to regard traders as partners in a cooperative venture (as, indeed, to some extent they are). Suppose, for example, that Smith buys seeds for one hundred dollars and expends six months' worth of effort growing a crop of tomatoes which he then trades to Jones for chickens that Jones raised from one hundred dollars' worth of chicks, expending six months' worth of effort in the process. Assume also that the effort in both cases is equally difficult, odious, effective, and so on. Then, clearly, Smith and Jones have both contributed equally to their common venture and have both

been rewarded equally, which means that the transaction was cooperatively fair.

The rub, of course, is in finding ways to determine such matters as the
relative effectiveness of various kinds of labor (recall those difficult
comparisons we listed earlier). In the made-up Smith and Jones example, we arbitrarily equated the effectiveness of their respective efforts,
so that we could then equate the values of the chickens and tomatoes
they traded. But how are we to determine the values of different sorts
of commodities in real life?[8]

One way, of course, is by means of market values. Using this way of
calculating, if the tomatoes in the Smith and Jones example can be readily sold in the marketplace for twice the price of the chickens, then
Smith's labor was twice as effective as was Jones's, so that their trade
has to be judged as not cooperatively fair. In a fair trade, Smith would
sell half his tomatoes for all of Jones's chickens.

Determining the effectiveness of labor in this way dovetails with the
broader idea, probably accepted by a majority of economists, that the
values, and thus the fair prices, of goods, capital, and labor are best determined by a genuinely free marketplace in which there are many competing players. An important virtue of this market approach for subjectivists is that market prices reflect the willingness of players to trade at
whatever the market prices happen to be, thus telling us the ways in
which actual John Does and Mary Roes value commodities.

But this way of looking at the matter, even considering only competitively fair marketplaces, has its problems. Perhaps the chief one is
that markets of this kind may reward not just foresight, risk taking, effort, and the like, factors that are relevant to determinations of cooperatively fair prices, but also "talents," such as economic power, that tend
to divide the benefits of trades in cooperatively unfair ways. We can
overcome this problem, to a large extent, by opting not merely for a
competitively fair marketplace but also for one that is completely
friendly. Prices in such a system, including the prices of labor and invested capital, would come as close as is possible to being cooperatively
fair. Taking this tack, however, would mean losing the practical advantages (in particular, efficiency) that make free enterprise systems attractive in the first place.

---

[8]If the trade is to make sense, Smith must value the chickens more highly than the tomatoes, and Jones vice versa. But it doesn't follow that the chickens and tomatoes therefore aren't equal in *market* value.

The obvious thought is that the best market system for those who value both fair play and efficiency would be one in which certain sorts of unfriendly competition (misrepresenting goods, forming monopolies, conspiring to set prices) are ruled out, while others are permitted, in particular those allowing astute players to take advantage both of shortages and of market gluts, including oversupplies of labor or venture capital. Resulting unfairnesses would then be rectified in various ways (governmental and/or philanthropic). For example, those paid much less than a cooperatively fair wage might be compensated by means of a negative income tax, while those receiving a good deal more could be reined in by steeply graduated income taxes and, so as also to level the playing field for the next generation, by severe inheritance and gift taxes. (Minimum wage laws probably aren't as good an idea, because experience seems to show that they tend to render unemployable those who are at the bottom of the labor pool and most in need of jobs. Maximum wage statutes may be a somewhat better idea, theoretically, but in practice they generally don't have much chance to be legislated.)[9]

The foregoing discussion underscores the point that there are no theoretical reasons for supposing that a socialistic economy is likely to be any more, or any less, cooperatively fair than a free enterprise economic system. It all depends on how a given system distributes the goods it produces. Socialists, of course, have argued otherwise. They see their kind of system as superior, for one reason, because it is easily wedded

---

[9]In the United States, there never has been a serious attempt to set a ceiling on wages or income. During World War II, President Roosevelt did propose a ceiling of twenty-five thousand dollars a year on salaries (a goodly sum in those days), the idea being that those who stayed at home should not profit while others were fighting and risking death defending the nation. His proposal never got off the ground because of immediate opposition by Congress, stemming from pressure exerted by fat cats. But in terms of the theory being championed here, his proposal made perfect sense. It was, in effect, an attempt on his part to make the rules of wartime economic games much friendlier than those existing in peacetime, so that the cooperative side of wartime social interactions would become more important than the competitive. Had the proposal been adopted, the competitive chances of soldiers, already hampered by having to fight overseas, would not have been additionally reduced by the tremendous disparities in their incomes vis-à-vis those of the citizens who remained at home. Note, by the way, that in days of old, soldiers who went off to war—and survived—generally plundered enough to do better financially than did stay-at-homes. This came much closer to being a cooperatively fair (that is, intraculturally fair!) arrangement than the one in effect in the United States during World War II.

to an egalitarian principle for the distribution of goods.[10] On the view championed here, however, egalitarianism is no virtue. Equal distributions cannot be fair unless—an impossible condition—everyone's labor happens to be equal in every respect to everyone else's.

This objection to economic egalitarianism applies also to the Marxist dictum: "From each according to his ability, to each according to his need." That principle, however, has quite a few other problems with it. For one thing, it fails to indicate how shirkers are to be treated. Do they receive according to their needs anyway? (The idea that there will be no shirkers in a truly socialistic society flies in the face of virtually everything experience tells us about human nature.) For another, there is no easy way to determine even approximately what the needs are of individual citizens. And for still another, the needs of some citizens are bound to conflict with those of others. We all, for example, have a need for positional goods that by their very nature only a few can possess.

But socialism does not necessarily imply egalitarianism. That the means of production are held in common, or that economic decisions are made by society as a whole, does not mean that those who work harder, or more effectively, or at more odious jobs, cannot be rewarded with greater shares of wealth, not to mention honor, fame, and the like, or that shirkers cannot be given much less.[11]

Of course, a socialistic system that employs a distribution principle based on merit faces the same problem as does a comparable free market system, namely, how to measure the relative effectiveness, odiousness, and so on, of different kinds of labor. So there is no theoretical difference with respect to cooperative fairness, any more than with respect to competitive fairness, between socialistic and free enterprise economic systems. A sensible fair-minded electorate will choose one system rather than the other, or more likely some particular combination of the two, on the basis of practical considerations, matters of taste, and feelings of compassion and in-group civility.

Before we leave the topic of economic fairness, three points need to

[10]One of the things that enraged so many citizens of Eastern European countries, and helped spark the overthrow of their communistic regimes, was the economic privilege of their ruling classes.

[11]Stalin's version of the Marxist distribution maxim, "From each according to his ability, to each according to his work," was not egalitarian, but from the point of view expressed here, it was a good deal fairer than the Marxist principle (not that the Soviet Union ever lived up to Stalin's).

be noted. First, the desire for fair play, stemming from reciprocal altruistic roots, often conflicts with other sorts of desire, including especially those whose origins are kin altruistic. The most important of these conflicts is probably the one between the natural desire to spend wealth on one's children (perhaps the most important reason for amassing even modestly large fortunes) and the desire to have a genuinely fair marketplace in which all players start out on the same footing. Unfortunately, conflicts of this kind generally cannot be resolved by merely theoretical considerations, because the strengths of the conflicting desires tend to differ from person to person. These conflicts have to be settled in the political arena, hopefully by fair procedures for coming to society-wide agreements.

Second, there is, alas, a sense in which a theoretical investigation of the kind undertaken here is bound to be discouraging. It isn't cheering to conclude that intuitions concerning fair play are as vague, as ambiguous, and even sometimes as contradictory as they have been characterized here. But we shouldn't forget that these limited sentiments nevertheless can serve as general guidelines, as they did with respect to the suggestions made above concerning ways for rendering overall economies reasonably fair without sacrificing market efficiency. In any case, the intuitions of some of us are sufficiently clear to tell us two extremely important facts about free market systems: first, that those at the bottom of the economic pecking order generally receive less than a fair return for their efforts; and second, that those at the top usually get far more. We don't need sharper intuitions in order to see that Henry George certainly was right in his claim that very few, if any, are those who have fairly earned (let's update his remark to account for inflation) fifty million dollars.

Third, there are many ways, in addition to the tax measures just mentioned, to offset the unfairnesses that seem to be inevitable side effects of any even modestly efficient free-market systems, without at the same time greatly reducing their efficiency. More strictly enforcing fair contracts and instituting genuinely competitively fair economic rules immediately come to mind. (In most, if not all, existing marketplaces, protection against chicanery is lax and the rules governing business practices favor some players at the expense of others.) But there also are measures that indirectly increase fair play by offsetting the political power that goes with large economic power. Examples are statutes that make it easier for ordinary citizens to vote and to collectively bargain through membership in honest unions, and measures making it easier for employees to own shares of the corporations in which they work. In addition, there are, of course, redistributive measures that can be employed to offset income maldistributions, including health and retirement insurance plans, measures providing opportunities to obtain the skills and knowledge required for economic success, and laws granting rights associated with the raising of children. The latter rights (e.g., guaranteed access to day care centers and time off from work to give birth) not only make an economic playing field more level but also help parents to raise children well, thus benefiting all of us in the long run.

Fairness and Justice

fair. . . . 8. Free of favoritism or bias; impartial. . . . 9. Just to all parties; equitable. . . . **Synonyms:** fair, just, equitable, impartial, unprejudiced, unbiased.
just. 1. Honorable and fair in one's dealings and actions. 2. Consistent with moral right; fair; equitable. . . . 4. Valid within the law; legitimate.

—*The American Heritage Dictionary*

justice. 1. Fairness. Equitableness. 2. Correct treatment. Merited reward or punishment. 3. . . . Correctness and impartiality in the application of the principles of rightness and of sound judgment. 4. The embodiment of the virtues (ideals, values, principles) of a society. 5. The establishment of harmony between one's rights and the rights of others (society, the public, government, or individuals). **justice, distributive.** . . . Allocating fairly to members of a community such things as money, property, privileges, opportunities, education, rights.

—Peter Angeles, *Dictionary of Philosophy*

So far in this work, the terms *fair* and *fairness* have occurred quite frequently, but not the terms *just* and *justice*. As used in everyday life and in legal and moral theory, these locutions, as well as their many variations, have become extremely ambiguous over the years, so that even their core senses tend to overlap, as the definitions that start this section indicate.

In his book *A Theory of Justice,* John Rawls explains his use of the phrase "justice as fairness," and his senses of both concepts, in this way:

> The original position [in which the basic laws of a society are to be chosen] is, one might say, the appropriate initial status quo, and thus the fundamental agreements reached in it are fair. This explains the propriety of

the name "justice as fairness": it conveys the idea that the principles of justice are agreed to in an initial situation that is fair. (p. 12)

It is very hard to know exactly what Rawls means by this, but presumably it is in part that the procedures by which the basic rules governing a society are chosen in the original position are fair in that they do not favor one citizen as compared to any others, and that justice results from such fair procedures. This suggests, although Rawls himself may not have meant it to, that it makes sense to call procedures *fair*, or *unfair*, and the outcomes of procedures *just*, or *unjust*.

Doing so has the merit of conforming to certain common usages. In everyday life, the terms "just" and "unjust," and their variants, often sound right when used with respect to the outcomes of trials although "fair" and "unfair" would sound wrong. It sounds right, for instance, to say that *justice* was done but wrong to say that *fairness* was done. Notice, however, that instead of speaking of justice being done, we can say that a decision or outcome was fair, as well as that it was fairly arrived at.[1]

When confronted with usage confusion of this kind, the important thing is to remain clear about the various kinds of things that need to be said using one or the other term. In this case, there are two general categories that need to be talked about, namely procedures and outcomes. It makes little difference which terms we use when discussing them, so long as we always are clear as to which sorts of cases we have in mind. Supposing, however, we adopt the convention that the terms "fair" and "unfair" are to apply to procedures and "just" and "unjust" to outcomes, then it would be right to say that a good deal of the earlier discussion in this treatise is about justice, as well as fairness. This is true in particular about chapter 10, which deals with desirable unfair outcomes, and chapter 15, concerned with economic fair play (which can be thought of as dealing with marketplace justice). Indeed, this work can (with some justice!) be characterized as a treatise on the nature of just social systems and the rational responses of fair minded citizens living in just, or unjust, societies.

---

[1] Interestingly, the prestigious *Encyclopedia of Philosophy,* edited by Paul Edwards (New York and London: MacMillan Publishing Company, 1967), has an entry under "Justice" but none under "Fairness." The article on justice, written by Stanley I. Benn, starts out by stating: "Although 'justice' is sometimes used as a synonym for 'law' or 'lawfulness,' it has a broader sense, closer to 'fairness.' "

The Good Person

A certain *man* went down from Jerusalem to Jericho, and fell among thieves, which stripped him of his raiment, and wounded *him,* and departed, leaving *him* for dead. And by chance there came down a certain priest that way; and when he saw him, he passed by on the other side. And likewise a Levite . . . But a certain Samaritan, as he journeyed, came where he was: and when he saw him, he had compassion *on him,* and went to *him,* and bound up his wounds, pouring in oil and wine, and set him on his own beast, and brought him to an inn, and took care of him. And on the morrow when he departed, he took out two pence, and gave *them* to the host, and said unto him, Take care of him; and whatsoever thou spendest more, when I come again, I will repay thee. Which now of these three, thinkest thou, was neighbour unto him that fell among the thieves?

—Luke 10:30–36

There are essentially three different kinds of sentiments motivating altruistic behavior: those favoring the making and keeping of fair agreements, those (for example, empathy and compassion) moving us to care about the welfare of others, and those that motivate sacrifices for close kin. Sentiments of the first kind evolved because they increased the likelihood of reciprocal altruism, the third because they fostered kin altruism, and the second for both of these reasons.

In this work, the twin concepts of morality and moral obligation have been characterized rather narrowly so as to cover only the first kind, thus qualifying as moral all of those who play the game of life fairly (by making and keeping fair contracts). Most philosophers, however, have had a somewhat broader conception of the moral person in mind, covering those individuals who are motivated by all three of the unselfish types of sentiments just mentioned. They often speak of an obligation

to be charitable, for example, and generally insist that we have an obligation to care for our own offspring. We need a broader concept that cov-
ers, more or less, what these other theorists have had in mind, in particular because being moral in the narrow sense—being scrupulously
honest—is not usually regarded as sufficient to merit the approval of
one's fellows. Even though the Scrooges of the world may honor contracts, obey the law, and so forth, they still are seen by others as miserable human specimens. Scrooge himself was not portrayed by Dickens
as a contract violator, but rather as a person whose lack of feelings for
others allowed him to take advantage of them in ways that were perfectly legal in his day, and perhaps even moral (in the narrow sense of
that term employed here). We look down on him, rather, because he was
a mean spirited, unfriendly person, unmotivated by the neighborly sentiments, exemplified by the biblical Good Samaritan, of compassion,
empathy, and a desire to help others in distress. He thus lacked what it
takes, let us say, to be a *good person*.

But being a good person is quite different from being goody-goody.
We can't just hate the sin while loving the sinner, as some philosophers
have proposed. Doctrines of universal love and forgiveness run counter
to deep-seated sentiments of the kind, for example, that were discussed
in chapter 5, above, concerning retribution and revenge. The good person (rare saints aside) is a full-blooded human being, capable of anger
and hatred as well as love, not a one-dimensional cardboard figure.
Good human beings have an *appropriate* stock of other-regarding sentiments and don't need to deny feelings of contempt, disdain, or hatred
directed towards deceitful, self-centered, selfish individuals.

This writer has lacked respect for most of the leaders of his native
land during his lifetime not only because they have so frequently played
the game unfairly but also because they have been so lacking in feeling
for fellow citizens in need. They have, in other words, been *bad* people.
The few who have gained this writer's respect are those who, although
frequently championing misguided policies, have nevertheless been
motivated in large part by feelings of empathy and compassion, and by
a sense of community encompassing all of their compatriots, not just
those on the top of the heap. My intent in espousing a theory of contractual fair play has not been to champion a dog-eat-dog morality. My
ideal world, in which better participants always emerge triumphant, is
not one in which competitive victors and those who are simply lucky
stand on a Nietzschean height and grind the rest of us into the dust.

18

Tit-for-Tat and the Prisoner's Dilemma

> The maxim "honesty is the best policy" is incomplete as it stands.
> Completed, it would read as follows: "Honesty is the best policy
> with those who are honest and the worst and stupidest policy with
> those who are dishonest."
> —Thomas Szasz (and several thousand others)

There has been a good deal written lately about whether so-called *prisoner's dilemmas* cast light on the evolution of moral behavior.[1] Here is an example that illustrates the essential features of this kind of dilemma:

> Two members of a criminal gang are arrested and imprisoned. Each prisoner is in solitary confinement with no means of speaking to or exchanging messages with the other. The police admit they don't have enough evidence to convict the pair on the principal charge. They plan to sentence both to a year in prison on a lesser charge. Simultaneously, the police offer each prisoner a Faustian bargain. If he testifies against his partner, he will go free while the partner will get three years in prison on the main charge. . . . [But] if *both* prisoners testify against each other, both will be sentenced to two years in jail. . . . In no case may either learn what the other has decided until he has irrevocably made his decision. Each is informed that the other . . . is being offered the very same deal. Each prisoner is concerned only with his own welfare—with minimizing his own sentence.[2]

---

[1]The game itself was invented by Merrill Flood and Melvin Dresher in 1950. Albert Tucker is responsible for the version dealing with prisoners, which has given the dilemma its catchy name. Perhaps the best book on the topic of prisoner's dilemmas is *The Evolution of Cooperation* by Robert Axelrod, with a chapter by W. D. Hamilton (New York: Basic Books, 1984).

[2]Taken from William Poundstone's excellent book, *Prisoner's Dilemma* (New York: Doubleday, 1992), p. 118. The other Poundstone quotes in this chapter are taken from that book. Poundstone also discusses several other games of some importance for evolution theory, including chicken, deadlock, stag hunt, and the free rider and volunteer's dilemmas.

In game theory lingo, refusing to testify is said to constitute "cooperation," and testifying, "defection."

The example nicely illustrates what makes a prisoner's dilemma a *dilemma,* for each player can reason as follows: "If my partner cooperates, then if I cooperate also, I'll have to serve a year in jail, whereas if I defect when he cooperates, I'll be set free. So if he cooperates, I'm better off defecting. On the other hand, if he defects and I cooperate, I'll get a three year sentence, whereas if I defect when he defects, I'll only be behind bars for two years. So if he defects, I'm better off defecting. *In either case, I'm better off defecting!*"

The trouble, of course, is that both players can reason in the same way, resulting in a double defection that earns them both two years in jail, whereas if both cooperate, they only have to serve one year.

The example constitutes a genuine prisoner's dilemma because it satisfies the technical conditions game theorists have specified. Payoffs are ordered so that defecting when the other party cooperates (the "temptation") provides the best payoff; mutual cooperation, the second best; mutual defection, the third; and cooperation when the other party defects (the "sucker's payoff"), the worst. The players must play the game, and they must choose either to cooperate or defect (they can't escape or bribe the authorities). They have no way of knowing whether the other party will cooperate or defect, nor can they make enforceable threats or commitments to the other party.

This example happens to be a *single-case* game; the two prisoners don't have to think about playing the game over and over. An *iterated* prisoner's dilemma is one in which two players engage in many single-case games, one after the other, without knowing which game is to be the last one. (To qualify as an iterated prisoner's dilemma, payoffs have to be ordered so that the reward for mutual cooperation is greater than the average of the temptation and the sucker's payoffs.) It has been proved that when players cannot trust each other, defection is the best strategy in single-case games, but in several iterated prisoner's dilemma tournaments, described by Robert Axelrod in his book *The Evolution of Cooperation,* in which various kinds of clever "strategies" were pitted against each other, the one that performed best overall turned out to be "*tit for tat,*" a relatively simple strategy requiring cooperation on the first play and, thereafter, imitation of whatever the other player has done on the previous play.[3] Most theorists have taken this result as evidence that when situations sufficiently like those constituting an iterated prisoner's dilemma occur in everyday life, the rational course of action for both players is to cooperate, so long as there is reciprocity, even supposing they have no regard for each other's welfare or for moral principles of fair play.

Some theorists go further and argue that these results shed light on the evolution of cooperative behavior between nonkin, of the kind that has been characterized here as reciprocal altruistic. W. D. Hamilton, for example, tried to show that genes favoring adoption of cooperative strategies like tit-for-tat could evolve within a population of defectors and that, once it did evolve, it would be robust (do well against other sorts of strategies) and stable (resist invasion by mutant strategies).[4]

But the question for us, here, is whether these theories about the evolution of cooperative behavior can account for, or explain, the evolution of *moral sentiments* favoring fair play, or explain why sentiments such as affection for nonkin might evolve. Hamilton's point is that among populations in which interactions resembling iterated prisoner's dilemmas occur with some frequency, genes favoring cooperation will arise and prosper; he doesn't prove that the evolving genes will tend to produce moral sentiments. They might just as well produce an increase in intelligence that enables organisms to see cooperation as often in their own best long-term interest. Indeed, in nature we find many sorts of reciprocal arrangements that have no moral aspect to them.

It still might be argued, of course, that if genes for moral sentiments did happen to arise in social populations, they would prosper because the kinds of cooperative behavior that solve iterated prisoner's dilemmas would thereby be increased. They would act as foils to the undoubtedly strong self-interested emotions tempting us to defect. This way of reasoning is supported by the fact that moral sentiments, having indeed evolved, must serve some biologically useful function. (No

---

[3]Recent investigations suggest that a slightly different strategy, called "Pavlov," is modestly superior to tit-for-tat. See the article "A strategy of win-stay, lose-shift that outperforms tit-for-tat in the Prisoner's Dilemma game," by Martin Nowak and Karl Sigmund, in *Nature* 364 (1 July 1993): 56–58. Even if this should turn out to be true, it will make no significant difference with respect to the discussion here.

[4]See the chapter written by Hamilton in *The Evolution of Cooperation*. Manfred Milinski, in a comment accompanying the *Nature* article by Nowak and Sigmund, just referred to, argues in much the same way, as do others.

repertoire that often includes personal sacrifice is likely to evolve unless it serves some genetic interest or other, however long run.) In the case of moral repertoire, it can be argued that the most plausible purpose its evolution served was to enable us to solve prisoner's dilemmas and thereby gain the long-term genetic benefits of cooperative ventures.[5]

The plausibility of this line of reasoning is enhanced when we concentrate on the problem posed by *single-case* prisoner's dilemmas. Recall that in these games, when sufficient trust is lacking, defection is the best strategy, even though mutual defection earns a smaller reward than does mutual cooperation. In the absence of trust, reason alone cannot solve single-case prisoner's dilemmas. But if the players have a moral sense, and can expect their partners also to be stocked with the relevant sentiments, then they can trust each other, and mutual cooperation becomes a rational choice.

This point can be put in another way by noticing that when players have a regard for fair play itself, or for their fellow players, prisoner's dilemmas turn into more benign games in which cooperation is the strategy most likely to maximize overall interests. The pain of guilt, the satisfaction gained by doing the morally right thing, or the pleasure at seeing the other player benefited can change the overall values of the various choice combinations so that situations cease to constitute prisoner's dilemmas. William Poundstone makes this point in his book *Prisoner's Dilemma:*

> [A] certain set of tangible payoffs is not enough to guarantee that a prisoner's dilemma exists. For a person with a sufficiently strong sense of empathy, there is no such thing as a prisoner's dilemma. The dilemma arises when two persons' preferences are ordered in a certain way. If your preferences never, ever, fit this pattern—if the "guilt" of betrayal outweighs the personal advantage gained *in every possible situation*— then you can never find yourself in a prisoner's dilemma. (Pp. 223–224)

Most of the prisoner's dilemma theorizing done by Axelrod and others has concerned two-person games, either of the single-case or the it-

---

[5]See, for example, James Q. Wilson's *The Moral Sense* (New York: The Free Press, 1993), pp. 66–69, and Katharine Milton's "Diet and Primate Evolution" (*Scientific American,* August, 1993), pp. 86–92. Milton argues, for example, that the evolution of primates, including *Homo sapiens,* subsisting on a high-protein, relatively low-bulk diet "required the *capacity to cooperate* with others (for instance, to communicate about who should run ahead of a hunted zebra and who behind), to defer gratification (to save food until it could be brought to an agreed site for all to share) and both to *determine one's fair portion* and to ensure that it was received" (italics added).

erated variety. But theorists have begun to consider prisoner's dilemmas concerning larger numbers of individuals, even whole societies, and what they say about these games also can be used to support the claim that moral sentiments evolved to solve prisoner's dilemmas. It is true that, in the old days (as today?), encounters involving many individuals probably tended not to satisfy the precise criteria defining multiple-person prisoner's dilemmas: threats must have been common, payoffs uncertain, play in a given game often not mandatory, and the responses of others, or their reputations, often known when the time came to act. Nevertheless, dilemmas very much like those constituting true multiple-person prisoner's dilemmas must have arisen quite frequently.

Free-rider dilemmas illustrate this point. The name derives from the problem confronting public transit riders when they can get away with not paying their fares. Here is Poundstone's example:

> It's late at night, and there's no one in the subway station. Why not just hop over the turnstiles and save yourself the fare? But remember, if *everyone* hopped the turnstiles, the subway system would go broke, and no one would be able to get anywhere.
>
> It is the easiest thing in the world to rationalize hopping the turnstiles. What's the chance that your lost fare will bankrupt the subway system? Virtually zero. . . . [B]ut if everybody thinks this way . . . (P. 126)

Daily life is full of situations in which benefits, large or small, can be gained by becoming a free rider, as, for example, when one person's walking on the grass does it no harm although everyone's doing so leads to its destruction.[6] In some cases, these dilemmas are true prisoner's dilemmas; in most, they resemble prisoner's dilemmas although they fail to satisfy all of the relevant technical criteria. The walking on the grass example illustrates this because, although payoffs generally are ordered as in the case of true prisoner's dilemmas, the fine-print criteria are not always satisfied (as they aren't, for example, when offenders can be reasonably sure most others will not follow suit).

It thus makes a good deal of sense to see the moral sentiments as having evolved as nature's way of solving problems posed by games at least very much like prisoner's dilemmas. When trust enters the picture,

---

[6] Even voting in large-scale elections presents a free-rider problem because it is in the interests of each voter not to vote (so as to save time, etc.), but if no one votes, representative government fails, and all suffer. (A person's vote counts in an election only if there is a tie vote or one's candidate loses by a single vote, both extremely unlikely outcomes in large-scale elections, a point made by Robert J. Ringer and others.)

prisoner's dilemmas turn into different sorts of games in which the payoffs favor cooperation rather than defection. But this can't have been the whole story. In the old days, large numbers of potentially cooperative interactions must have occurred, as they do today, in which the payoffs were significantly different from those of true prisoner's dilemmas. The games people play are of many different kinds.

Volunteer's dilemmas, multiple-person variations on the well-known game of *chicken,*[7] are perhaps the most important of these other games. Volunteer's dilemmas resemble the free-rider variety, indeed the two kinds of games blend into each other in borderline cases. Pure instances, however, differ in two ways: (1) free-rider success hinges on the cooperation of all or most other players, whereas those who neglect to volunteer generally need the cooperation of only one or a very few other players; and (2) the payoffs of the two kinds of games are somewhat different (as will become evident shortly).

The important difference between volunteer's and prisoner's dilemmas is in the ordering of payoffs. The sucker's payoff (the return for cooperating when the others defect) in a prisoner's dilemma is smaller than the reward for mutual defection, but larger in the case of volunteer's dilemmas. Suppose, for example, that phone and electric power lines in the neighborhood go out during a blizzard. The telephone and electric companies will send workers out to fix the problem, *provided* they are notified of the service interruptions. So someone in the neighborhood has to make the trek to the nearest working telephone. But it's always better if the other guy expends the effort.

Of course, when the power goes out, the stakes aren't all that high in the great sweep of things. But volunteer's dilemma stakes can be very high indeed. In wartime, for instance, it generally is in the interests of each soldier to have someone else volunteer for dangerous duty, but if no one volunteers, the consequences for all are likely to be dire.[8]

The important point to notice about the multiple-person dilemmas just discussed is that they share two crucial features with two-person prisoner's dilemmas: (1) *defection pays better than cooperation when others cooperate,* and (2) *mutual cooperation provides a better payoff*

---

[7]Chicken dilemmas differ crucially from prisoner's dilemmas because mutual defection (neither player "chickening out") provides the worst, indeed often a life-threatening, payoff.

[8]According to game theorist Anatol Rapoport, the natives of Tierra del Fuego have a word that means "looking at each other hoping that either will offer to do something that both parties desire but are unwilling to do." Volunteer's dilemmas crop up everywhere.

than mutual defection. Moral and other-regarding sentiments thus can be seen as having evolved, in part, to increase the likelihood of cooperation in these situations, counterbalancing selfish motives that urge defection. The idea, mentioned at the start of this chapter, that the study of prisoner's dilemmas casts light on the evolution of moral sentiments, thus can be seen as not quite on the mark, for it makes better sense to see moral sentiments as having evolved because they help solve all sorts of dilemmas in which, otherwise, the payoffs would be ordered in the devilish way just described. (This line of reasoning also explains the evolution of sentiments favoring retribution. When retribution enters the scene, the likely payoffs for defection become negative, sometimes life threatening [e.g., expulsion from the group, or capital punishment] and thus smaller than the sucker's payoff.)

Before leaving this topic, a note of caution is in order. The number of games that people can, and sometimes do, play is extremely large. Game theory is still in its infancy. In this chapter, we haven't considered cases (to mention only the most obvious) in which force, or stealth, enter the picture; defection is partial rather than total; organized groups engage in in-group betrayal; or "golden opportunities" (opportunities to cheat when the chances of getting caught are very low) tempt dishonest behavior.[9] Nevertheless, it seems very likely that the moral sentiments evolved in part in order to solve the problems posed by games, such as prisoner's and volunteer's dilemmas, in which, in the absence of trust, the payoffs are arranged so that either defection pays better than cooperation when others cooperate or mutual cooperation provides a better payoff than mutual defection.

---

[9]Robert H. Frank's *Passions Within Reason* (New York: W.W. Norton, 1988) contains an interesting discussion of golden opportunities. Note, however, that taking advantage of golden opportunities becomes cheating, or theft, rather than simply acquisition, only against a backdrop of a system reflecting widely shared moral sentiments.

The Appeal of Some Noncontractarian Moral Theories

> There are fewer things in heaven and earth than are dreamt of by the philosophers.
>
> — Harry Gardener (and others)

One of the problems in deciding among the various kinds of moral theories that have been proposed over the years is that so many of them seem plausible even though they tend to be incompatible with each other. This poses an especially serious problem for ethical subjectivists because it raises the question as to how we can have sentiments favoring such a diversity of moral principles. Wherein lies the appeal of these incompatible moral standards?

In some cases, the answer no doubt lies in the wishful thinking or self-deception that so often clouds judgment and masks some of our deepest sentiments and desires. Moral principles that require us to act out of love for all human beings (championed, for instance, by Joseph Fletcher) are a case in point. We may like to think that we want to be as we picture the Mother Teresas of the world, but in fact we do not. It isn't simply that we don't love everyone, but rather that we don't even desire to. Universal love is not held, genuinely, even as an ideal standard by more than, at most, the tiniest number of human beings. As Richard Dawkins remarked, "Much as we might wish to believe otherwise, universal love and the welfare of the species as a whole are concepts which simply do not make evolutionary sense."[1]

In other cases, the apparent plausibility of moral principles derives from their appeal to other-regarding, but nonmoral sentiments, in par-

---

[1] *The Selfish Gene*, pp. 2–3.

ticular to those of compassion and empathy. This may well be the case, for example, with respect to animal rights theories, such as the one championed by Peter Singer.

But in a great many cases, the appeal of noncontractarian theories lies in their resemblance to contractual systems of the type championed here, or at least in their not contradicting that sort of theory. Consider the following examples.

The Golden Rule   The Golden Rule is one of the oldest, simplest, and most widely appealing of all moral principles: "As ye would that men should do to you, do ye to them likewise" (positive version), or "As ye would not that men should do to you, likewise do not to them" (negative version). The Golden Rule sometimes is dismissed as rather silly, on the grounds that we often would that others treat us in ways we know to be unfair or preferential, say by forgiving us our sins rather than punishing us for them. But these quick rejections miss the point of this precept, which is that just as others should treat us fairly, or justly, so also we should deal with them.

Regarded in this way, the Golden Rule is rather low in normative content, since it doesn't spell out the details concerning what fair, or just, treatment consists in. Even so, it has three virtues that make it attractive: it reminds us that morality requires the just, or fair, treatment of others; it suggests that just treatment is the same for others as for us; and, more importantly, it exhorts us to treat others fairly. Because it doesn't tell us what justice or fairness consists in, virtually all more-or-less standard moral theories, certainly all that are contractual in nature, are compatible with the Golden Rule. The great appeal of this precept thus does not count against the moral principles championed in this work.

The Universalization Principle   The universalization principle often is expressed in the query "What if everyone did that?" If everyone did do that—walk on the grass, use too much hot water in wartime Britain, two stock examples—the consequences would be bad for all concerned, even though, if others do not and you do, the consequences would be good for you while not harming others. In some cases, such as walking on the grass when others are likely to notice, the harm (damaged grass) results if other people are motivated to do so in turn. But in others, say using too much hot water in a private bath, what you do need have no effect on anyone else's actions. Where, then, is the harm in your doing these things? On purely consequentialist (outcome, teleological, forward-looking) theories, such as utilitarianism, it is hard to see how this question can be answered.

But from the contractualist point of view defended here, there is an immediate answer. In World War II Britain, if everyone had used large quantities of hot water, it might indeed have affected the war effort in a serious way, whereas one person's doing so would not have. The person who used lots of hot water, knowing that most others did not, thereby took advantage of—gained an advantage over—those who patriotically refrained. Our instinctive reaction, as *cooperating competitors,* is to see this sort of action by a fellow cooperator as competition that is unfair because contrary to society-wide agreements, thus violating one of the two fundamental principles of fairness championed in this work. And that may account for a good deal of the appeal of this little slogan.

Note, by the way, the related principle embodied in the query, "What if everyone else *does* do that?" Although philosophers have not paid much attention to this principle, the fact that all, or most, or even many fellow citizens violate a law or custom often is seen in daily life as justification for doing so in turn—the more widespread or serious the infringement, the greater the justification. Philosophers often scoff at this sort of defense, seeing it as a rationalization that cannot possibly justify what otherwise would be an immoral action. And yet, that most others cheat on their income taxes, or ignore signs to keep off the grass, does indeed tend to remove the stigma from someone else's also doing so (as we argued in chapter 12). Obedience to generally ignored social rules may well be meritorious (perhaps because it sets a good example), but it goes beyond what is required by the dictates of morality. The failure of all or most citizens to live up to agreements releases others from the obligation to comply in return. Lack of reciprocity earns lack of reciprocity.[2]

Cultural Relativism   The point of the wise saying "When in Rome do as the Romans do" is not just prudence; there usually is something morally right in doing things the way others do. There is, after all, great

---

[2]Many textbooks on good and bad reasoning, including two authored by this writer, discuss a fallacy sometimes called "Two wrongs make a right" in which an otherwise wrong action is "justified" by citing a similar wrong done by others, as when a South African responds to an American's condemnation of apartheid by pointing to racial discrimination in the United States. In these cases, however, the wrong being "justified" is not done in response to the other wrong; it is not a case of "fighting fire with fire."

benefit in having socially mandated ways of acting in various kinds of situations. It doesn't matter, for example, whether we drive on the left or the right side of the road; what matters is that we agree to drive on one side or the other and then drive on that side.

But cultural relativists go overboard when they argue that there are no ways to determine moral right and wrong other than by appeal to cultural standards, and they surely must be mistaken in their claim that social standards cannot be immoral.

Nevertheless, cultural relativism dovetails with contractarianism at least to this extent: both kinds of theories assert that what makes many actions obligatory, or forbidden, is that the group has agreed, implicitly or explicitly, to do things in certain ways. So in spite of its serious wrongheadedness, cultural relativism has something right about it; hence, perhaps, a large part of its appeal.

Utilitarianism   Forms of utilitarianism that implicitly require us to take account of the consequences of our actions on human beings all over the world, and not just on in-group members, have little to say for themselves from the point of view of a biologically based contractual theory. Biological theory strongly denies that any but the tiniest minority of us could possibly have the sentiments required to make it rational for us to sacrifice in the way that this form of utilitarianism requires for people we don't know and with whom we have had not the slightest contact, a denial that is very well supported by introspection and by observations of ourselves and others in action.[3]

But there are other versions of utilitarianism that properly take the in-group/out-group nature of human beings into account, at least implicitly. John Rawls provides us with such a version (which he then proceeds to criticize, being himself a social contract theorist): "Society is rightly ordered, and therefore just, when its major institutions are arranged so as to achieve the greatest net balance of satisfaction summed up over all the individuals belonging to it."[4] This is perhaps the most defensible version of the utilitarian principle, but it too is defective, at least from the contractualist (or any deontological—backward-looking) point of view. However, given that legions of writers, including Rawls, have covered

---

[3]The best way to maximize worldwide utility may well be to forego all non-necessities and instead, say, buy food and send it to starving children somewhere or other in the world.

[4]In *A Theory of Justice,* p. 22.

this territory rather thoroughly, there is little need here to till this very well plowed ground once again.

But perhaps it should be mentioned here that even when restricted to in-group matters, utilitarianism runs counter to a basic fact about human nature suggested by evolution theory: virtually all human beings lack sufficient interest in the *end* that utilitarianism promotes, namely, the maximization of in-group human satisfaction *without regard to how that satisfaction is distributed.* Theory suggests, and experience confirms, that most of us see some people in society as more deserving than others (following the principles of fair play discussed in this work) and have a greater interest in our own satisfaction and that of close kin, friends, and other acquaintances than we do in the general run of people in our culture.

The question here, however, is not what is wrong with utilitarianism but rather why it nevertheless has a certain amount of appeal, even for contractualists. Why should a theory that focuses on overall social welfare be attractive? The answer, very likely, is, first, that our own welfare is closely tied to that of the group as a whole—we tend to prosper when the group does and to suffer when it suffers (recall the discussion in chapter 2 concerning genetic winners)—and, second, that most of us have a modest amount of empathy and concern for other in-group members, seeing their benefit as desirable, although this obviously is less true with respect to large or heterogeneous societies than in those that are small and cohesive. (Recall earlier remarks in chapter 6 about societies being somewhat like very large friendship groups.)

Kant's Categorical Imperatives "Act only on that maxim which you can at the same time will that it should become a universal law" (first version). "So act as to treat humanity, whether in your own person or in that of any other, in every case as an end, never as a means only" (second version). Kant claimed that these two principles are merely different formulations of the same imperative (as also the third version, not considered here), but in fact they are logically distinct (the reason they are labeled above as his "categorical imperative*s*"). Although Kant's ethical position is usually thought of as contractual (Rawls, for instance, characterizes it in this way), none of Kant's categorical imperatives has an explicitly contractual component in it.

This writer confesses to being somewhat mystified by the immense popularity and respect with which Kant's ethical position is generally regarded by most moral theorists.[5] But it has two features that he would like to think account for at least some of its popularity. One is that his first version of the categorical imperative requires all of one's moral principles to be consistent, both in themselves and with each other, and this also is required, or at least held as an ideal, by virtually all contractarian theories. The other is that his second version requires what would be required by a completely friendly social contract. The second version tells us always to treat others as ends, never just as means, which in our lingo translates into the principle never to take advantage of others, a precept that carries to an extreme ideas concerning very friendly competition discussed in chapter 6.

Natural Rights Theories   No subjectivist can accept the idea that there are "natural" rights or obligations, if for no other reason than the lack of any perceived features of the universe to which the alleged natural rights or duties might correspond. What, then, accounts for the popularity of natural rights theories?

Perhaps the explanation lies in the tendency we all have, encouraged by linguistic conventions, to reify—to project onto the external world— personal attitudes or responses to various kinds of abstract, or subjective, entities. We reify when, for example, we assert, with literal intent, that moldy food is disgusting; that a landscape is beautiful, or ugly; that filet mignon tastes better than smoked salmon; or that determining *the* meaning of life is a deep philosophical problem; when, in fact, *we* are disgusted by the mold or mildew; *we* like the taste of filet mignon bet-

---

[5]The most important reasons for this mystification are that (1) Kant derives the second version of his categorical imperative, which after all states an idea voiced countless times prior to his day, by means of a horrendous logical blunder (reasoning from the idea that every rational being considers its own existence as an end in itself, to the conclusion that every rational being should treat all rational beings as ends in themselves— try rendering that argument into anything remotely like the notation of Russellian predicate logic and its invalidity becomes apparent); (2) his first version boils down merely to the obvious idea that moral principles should be consistent; (3) his examples intended to illustrate the first version do not apply that imperative correctly, making use of human desires in contradiction to Kant's vehement and repeated insistence that they are irrelevant; and (4), he overlooks the fact that the first version, while a necessary, or at least an ideal, condition for almost any rational ethical system (because it forbids acceptance of inconsistent moral principles), is surely not sufficient, given that an infinite number of moral principles would satisfy it. In remarking on the fact that Kant seems not to have noticed this, C.D. Broad states (in his *Five Types of Ethical Theory*): "This is of course absolutely indefensible, and charity bids us turn our eyes from the painful spectacle," a remark with which this writer finds himself in complete agreement.

ter than smoked salmon; *we* find landscapes beautiful (beauty being in the eye of the beholder) or ugly; and the philosophical problem we all face is to figure out what life means to *us*.[6] Perhaps natural rights theorists have simply given in to this natural reification tendency, which explains not just what is wrong with their position—there is no *the* meaning of life, and no heat in a hot stove (although there are rapidly moving molecules that cause the feeling of heat in *us*), and, similarly, there are no objective natural rights or duties—but also why so many people find their theory attractive. It lets them see the privileges they would like to have, and perhaps want to grant others, and the duties they are willing to accept, and to demand that others be bound by, as natural—as part of the objective features of the universe rather than just the way that they feel about moral matters.

Interestingly, a great many of the particular rights and obligations often seen as natural correspond to internal sentiments felt by most human beings. It is also interesting that disputes among natural rights theorists often concern cases in which intuitions tend to be vague, ambiguous, or contradictory.

---

[6]Of course, in everyday life, and even when doing theoretical investigations, we sometimes use reifying locutions without meaning them literally, as when someone says that a play is wonderful but means merely to express a personal response to it.

John Rawls's Social Contract Theory

. . . [T]he capacity for a sense of justice and the moral feelings is an adaption of mankind to its place in nature. . . . [T]he behavior patterns of a species, and the psychological mechanisms of their acquisition, are just as much of its characteristics as are the distinctive features of its bodily structures; and these patterns of behavior have an evolution exactly as organs and bones do. It seems clear that for members of a species which lives in stable social groups, the ability to comply with fair cooperative arrangements and to develop the sentiments necessary to support them is highly advantageous, especially when individuals have a long life and are dependent on one another. These conditions guarantee innumerable occasions when mutual justice consistently adhered to is beneficial to all parties.

—John Rawls

John Rawls's rather repetitive and tedious, but nevertheless extremely insightful and interesting books, *A Theory of Justice* and *Political Liberalism,* contain what is very likely the most discussed contract theory proposed in the twentieth century.[1] In both works, he restricts his discussion to political philosophy, saying next to nothing about moral precepts except as they relate to his ideas concerning the just society.

The basic thrust of his thought that is of concern here is very similar in both books, although each book concentrates on different aspects of his theory. He wants to show what the basic political principles and institutions of a just society would be like, and he derives and justifies a particular set of standards, liberties, and rights in roughly the same way

---

[1]John Rawls, *A Theory of Justice* (Cambridge: Harvard University Press, 1971), and *Political Liberalism* (New York: Columbia University Press, 1993). All quotations of Rawls in this chapter are from these two books.

in both books: via hypothetical deliberations among citizens deprived of certain kinds of information about themselves. In *A Theory of Justice,* however, he assumes that his bargainers are free and rational agents in a "well ordered society" in which there is general agreement about basic moral beliefs and the good life. He admits that his political theory might need to be revised "once these other matters [personal morality] are understood." In *Political Liberalism,* he tries to take account of the fact that the citizens of modern nations differ greatly with respect to their religious, moral, and philosophical convictions, and he limits his discussion to liberal democratic societies, trying to show what a liberal society that could gain the assent of *reasonable*, as opposed to just rational, citizens would be like. Reasonable citizens are assumed to have a desire to cooperate fairly with others so disposed on terms taking account of the differences in goals and beliefs of the various parties, whereas rational agents, as the phrase is used in *Political Liberalism,* are not presumed to have such a desire. In that book, Rawls proposes a "political conception" that reasonable citizens will see as "derived from, or congruent with, or at least not in conflict with, their other values."

Although our topics only partially overlap, Rawls's theory is similar to mine in many respects. He assumes, for example, that the moral side of human nature has "an evolution exactly as organs and bones do" (a point neglected by most of the host of his commentators); he sees society as "a cooperative venture for mutual advantage" in which, however, cooperators also are competitors; and he conceives of political justice in terms of fair contractual arrangements that facilitate cooperative activities. In addition, his conception of individuals who are reasonable, while different from mine about rational agents who are fair-minded, is sufficiently like it so that, in a sense, both of our theories constitute proposals about societies fair-minded rational individuals might endorse.

His theory, however, is less broad in scope than mine. It deals primarily with "strict," as opposed to "partial," compliance theory (concerned with punishment, etc.) and, as just mentioned, it says next to nothing about moral problems outside of the range of political philosophy.

Rawls sees a just society as one whose social life is governed by basic laws that would be agreed to by "free and rational persons concerned to further their own interests" deliberating without knowledge either of their own positions in society (class, social status, etc.), or of their own intelligence and strengths, or even of their own preferences and psychological propensities (including those that are moral) other than those common to most persons (for example, a preference for primary goods).

He thinks that citizens in this "original position" would choose two "principles of justice" to govern their society: (1) "Each person is to have an equal right to the most extensive total system of equal basic liberties compatible with a similar system of liberty for all"; and (2) "Social and economic inequalities are to be arranged so that they are both: (a) to the greatest benefit of the least advantaged [the "difference principle"], consistent with the just savings principle [requiring that the interests of future generations be taken into account], and (b) attached to offices and positions open to all under conditions of fair equality and opportunity." They also, Rawls says, would choose "priority rules" indicating, roughly speaking, that a given liberty cannot be restricted except for the sake of a more extensive liberty (majority rule being the most extensive liberty); that "a less than equal liberty must be acceptable to those with the lesser liberty"; that any inequality of opportunity must improve the chances of those with the lesser opportunity; and that "an excessive rate of savings must on balance mitigate the burden of those bearing this hardship."

These principles and priority rules are intended to spell out more precisely the content of a "General Conception" stating that: "All social primary goods—liberty and opportunity, income and wealth, and the bases of self-respect—are to be distributed equally unless an unequal distribution of any or all of these goods is to the advantage of the least favored."

After his deliberators choose these principles and priority rules, Rawls has them move on to a second stage, where they choose a constitution for their society in which basic liberties are specified that guarantee, for example, the right to vote and to be eligible for public office, freedom of speech and assembly, freedom of thought, the right to hold personal property, and freedom from arbitrary arrest and seizure. (He then has them proceed to a third and a fourth stage not dealt with here.)

One might object to Rawls's theory on grounds that those in the original position would not choose the principles or liberties Rawls thinks they would. But our concern here is, first, to show how the principles and liberties he has them choose compare, both in content and in the way they are justified, with the principles of fair competition and cooperation championed in this work; second, to argue that, where different, Rawls's principles and his methods of justification are less satisfactory; and third, to attempt to explain at least in part why so many people have found his theory attractive.

Rawls's First Principle of Justice is consistent with my view of fair play in granting to everyone an *equal* right to the most extensive possible set of basic liberties. But it differs, when spelled out in the constitutional stage, because it guarantees liberties or rights, in particular the right to hold property, that according to my theory are not required by moral considerations (although they may be compatible with them).

Rawls's Second Principle of Justice also is consistent in many ways with my fair play principles, in particular in guaranteeing fair opportunity to everyone. But it differs by allowing goods to be distributed unequally only when this is to the greatest benefit of those least well off. It thus is more egalitarian than my meritarian standard.[2]

His theory also differs from mine in seeing the garnering of a greater-than-average share of goods, even under conditions of fair opportunity, as morally undeserved when due to better natural endowment (e.g., intelligence). He takes this position because he believes that natural endowment is morally undeserved. On my view, natural endowment is irrelevant to questions concerning the fair distribution of goods. (Recall, however, the earlier discussion, in particular in chapter 15, about what the successful owe others for providing education, protection, opportunities for success, and the like.)

Note also that the priority rules Rawls specifies, while again consistent in some ways with my principles of fair play, differ from them in others. In particular, his priority rules are more egalitarian and require that a less-than-equal liberty be permitted only by agreement with those having the lesser liberty. (If taken literally, by the way, the latter would proscribe institution of a wartime draft if some of those to be chosen to serve did not agree to have their liberty thus reduced.) As to the rights and freedoms he has those in the second stage select, all but two are implied by my theory. One of these two, freedom from arbitrary searches and seizures, clearly would be chosen by any fair-minded electorate. But the other, the right to hold private property, is not implied by my

---

[2]It is unclear just how egalitarian Rawls's position really is. Does he mean to say that every economic change merely has to increase goods for those at the bottom of the heap or rather that every change must increase goods for those at the bottom to a greater degree than for others in society? If the former, then his principles of justice would not rule out the possibility of immense differences in wealth arising between rich and poor. If the latter, then his just society would be one in which after a period of time everyone would have an equal share in the goods society has to offer. Presumably, Rawls believes that the circumstances in actual societies would make his difference principle modestly egalitarian in practice.

theory, nor is it clear that a fair-minded electorate would always and under every normal circumstance vote for such a right.

In general, Rawls's theory is like mine with respect to competitive fairness and in that he does not justify his claim that the conditions specified for the original position are fair by an appeal to any objective considerations or metaphysical arguments. However, his claim that the standards agreed to in the original position are just because the conditions existing there are designed so as to produce pure procedural justice is altogether different from anything said in my theory.

Pure procedural justice, he says, results when we have no independent criterion for evaluating an outcome, but the fair procedure employed guarantees that whatever results is just. His example is a gambling situation in which the rules are competitively fair, so that the resulting outcome, unknowable in advance, will be just. He distinguishes pure procedural justice from the perfect variety, rare in important cases, obtained when "there is an independent criterion for what is a fair division," and also from imperfect procedural justice (illustrated by fair court trials), obtained when "there is an independent criterion for the correct outcome, [but] . . . no feasible procedure which is sure to lead to it."

Rawls believes that our moral sentiments, in particular those concerning cooperative fairness and cooperative justice, are too vague and incomplete to justify a selection of basic social governing principles, but that the conditions specified for the original position guarantee that the standards selected will yield pure procedural justice. On my view, our moral sentiments are rather sharp concerning competitive fairness and, while certainly vague concerning fair divisions of cooperative efforts, are sufficiently substantive to guide us in the selection of broad general standards governing social intercourse. It also seems to me that where intuitions are unclear, there is no reason to suppose that merely deciding by means of fair competitive procedures will assure cooperative fair play. (On this score, recall James Fishkin's claim that there are no procedures which guarantee just outcomes.)

Finally, note that Rawls's theory, as expounded in *Political Liberalism,* deals only with justice in a liberal democratic society, whereas mine concerns political systems of any kind and deals with individuals under every sort of condition. Note also that Rawls does not explicitly justify restricting what he says in *Political Liberalism* in this way. One implication of this restriction is that there are other possible political systems that are just, but according to my theory, the basic principles of fair play do not differ from one kind of society to another.

Let's turn now to the principal reasons for my belief that Rawls's theory, while excellent in many ways, is not quite on the mark. (A few other reasons are implied by what has already been said.) To start with, it seems to me that Rawls's assertion that we do not deserve gains obtained via superior native ability is in error. If he were right, no one would ever deserve anything, since all productivity is influenced by native talents.[3]

It also seems to me that Rawls's thought-experiment involving the original position is misconceived. Although in some places Rawls strongly asserts that deciding under the conditions specified for the original position would produce pure procedural justice, what he says elsewhere indicates that at best this would only partly be true. When justifying his claim about the original position he says that it "both expresses reasonable conditions and *yields principles which match our considered judgments duly pruned and adjusted* " (italics added). This implies, in particular when coupled with several other remarks, that his intent was to stipulate conditions so that deliberations in the original position would yield standards which he himself finds intuitively right and which he thinks other fair-minded persons would see in the same way, so that there are indeed independent criteria for evaluating the standards chosen in the original position. At best, then, the principles chosen there can only partly constitute pure procedural justice. Perhaps, however, the thought-experiment concerning the original position is just a way for Rawls, and other fair-minded people, to sharpen and broaden their previously held moral sentiments, *a la* Nelson Goodman's well known dictum, "A rule is amended if it yields an inference we are unwilling to accept; an inference is rejected if it violates a rule we are unwilling to amend," which Rawls mentions in the relevant place in his discussion. If at bottom this is what he is up to, then it seems to me that his use of the device of a hypothetical original position is neither a good idea nor (either in his case or mine) necessary.[4] If the aim is to broaden and sharpen sentiments concerning principles of *justice,* then the right thought-experiment would be one in which the deliberators consult

---

[3]It also seems to me that Rawls's position here gets him into trouble on an issue related to that of free will versus determinism. But discussion of that topic is beyond the scope of this work.

[4]The point is complicated by the fact that in *Political Liberalism* Rawls has his bargainers be not just rational but also reasonable, where the latter term carries the moral freight previously mentioned.

their own sentiments concerning justice, moving back and forth between rules and particular cases, while trying to blot out thoughts concerning their own nonmoral interests, rather than attempting to maximize their own chances.

But perhaps the most important disagreement between us has to do with his difference principle, particularly if he intends it to be a somewhat egalitarian principle. In my opinion, although there is something in most of us that responds to egalitarian ideas, most fair-minded people who carefully consider particular cases, making an effort to discount personal circumstances and prospects, will favor a meritarian standard. (Of course, if Rawls intends his difference principle to be construed so that immense disparities in wealth would be possible, then in my opinion, the difference principle is way off the mark.)

Why then has Rawls's theory been received so favorably? One reason, perhaps, is that most of the principles, liberties, and rights he has those in the original position select are at least modestly similar to the standards many others justify on other grounds. Another reason is that he has proposed a social contract theory, and supported it by an at least implied appeal to moral sentiments rather than to metaphysical argument. (This writer, of course, likes Rawls's nod in the direction of evolutionary biology.) It also is true that egalitarianism has a certain amount of attractiveness (about which more will be said in chapter 24).

Finally, the appeal of Rawls's theory may result in part from the fact that he always is completely level-headed and that what he has to say is so obviously based on a good deal of insight into how the human psyche works its will in the sociopolitical arena.

21

Robert Nozick's Libertarian Natural Rights Theory

. . . [A] minimal state, limited to the narrow functions of protection against force, theft, fraud, enforcement of contracts, and so on, is justified; . . . any more extensive state will violate persons' rights not to be forced to do certain things, and is unjustified; . . . the minimal state is inspiring as well as right.

—Robert Nozick

Ratio of compensation paid Allied Signals CEO last year to wages paid its 3,810 Mexican *maquiladora* workers: 3:2

—"Harper's Index" item (August 1995)

Robert Nozick's National-Book-Award-winning *Anarchy, State, and Utopia*[1] has very likely received more attention than any other recently published moral tract, excepting only John Rawls's *A Theory of Justice* just discussed. The chief features of Nozick's position are these four: (1) a "Lockean natural rights" starting point; (2) the claim that what he calls a "minimal state" is justified (because it could have arisen from a state of nature via voluntarily-joined "protective associations" that became minimal states, without violating anyone's Lockean natural rights); (3) the claim that no other, more extensive, state is justified (because it could not have arisen justly from a state of nature without violating someone's Lockean natural rights); and (4) his "entitlement" theory of distributive justice derived from his natural rights starting point.

The gist of Nozick's Lockean natural rights moral underpinning (not counting economic principles to be discussed later) is this: In a state of

---

[1]Robert Nozick, *Anarchy, State, and Utopia* (New York: Basic Books, 1974). All quotations of Nozick in this chapter are from this book.

nature, individuals have freedom of action and can dispose of their possessions as they see fit, within the bounds of the "law of nature," which requires that (in Locke's words) "no one ought to harm another of his life, health, liberty or possessions." Those injured by a transgression of these bounds may defend themselves against this invasion of their rights, recover damages, and have the transgressors punished (proportionately to the seriousness of the crime) so as to deter further transgressions. Nozick sees this moral structure as constructing a "boundary" of rights around each person, so that any "boundary crossings" are wrong and, in a just state, are forbidden (except, for instance, when restitution is made).

Most natural rights theories are held by their proponents as objective theories justified not by appeal to internal sentiments or preferences but rather by a claim that they are moral laws of nature of one sort or another. Nozick doesn't directly discuss the question of objectivity versus subjectivity, but the general tone of his writings supports the idea that he holds his version of Lockean natural rights to be objective. If this is his view, then we have here a fundamental difference between his theory and mine, and he needs to address at least the major objections raised against all objective moral theories (e.g., of the kind discussed by J. L. Mackie in his book *Ethics: Inventing Right and Wrong*).[2] On the other hand, if he believes that his Lockean starting point can be defended by an appeal to moral sentiments, then our disagreement has to do with the nature of the relevant sentiments held by most people, a point that will be more evident in what is said later concerning his "entitlement" theory.

Nozick also insists that no state more comprehensive than a minimal state can be legitimate. In the real world, of course, even a state confined to the tasks of protecting its citizens and enforcing legitimate contracts — the only tasks Nozick allows to a minimal state — would very likely have to become quite extensive indeed. Think only of the military-industrial complex in the United States today or of the vast American law enforcement, justice, and prison systems. What sorts of activities, then, does he think a full-blown state cannot engage in without violating citizens' natural rights? One kind, at least implied by his theory, is that it cannot institute rules that interfere with the procurement or use of private property, except when it does so to prevent unjustified boundary crossings. It cannot, for instance, institute zoning laws forbidding land

---

[2]J. L. Mackie, *Ethics: Inventing Right and Wrong* (Harmondsworth, Middlesex, England: Penguin Books, 1977).

uses that do not interfere with anyone else's natural rights. Another is that it cannot justly institute genuinely redistributive policies; it cannot enact "entitlement" or "welfare" regulations.

Although there is a modest similarity between Nozick's claim about redistributive principles and my own thoughts on the matter, there is an important difference. Nozick holds that a state is justified in taxing its citizens (taking wealth from them) only to the extent that taxes amount to fees for services rendered. My view, as explained in chapter 14, is that taxes are *outcome-fair* only if they are fees for services rendered, but that an outcome-unfair tax is *procedurally fair* if chosen by a fair decision procedure. So on my view, contrary to Nozick's, a tax that is not for services rendered may be fairly enacted and in that way be fair (thus having a certain amount of moral binding force on fair-minded citizens). In addition, on my view, taxes unfair in themselves may counter other social unfairnesses, and thus tend to make a whole social system fairer than it would otherwise be.

Unfortunately, Nozick says very little about how protective associations that become minimal states are to be governed. What he does say, however, implies that the procedures of dominant protective associations would be determined by the owners of those organizations. If this really is his view, then it would seem to make clients virtual captives of the association owners, with little recourse other than flight. (Nozick never explains why those who run successful protective associations would not turn their organizations into tyrannical state oligarchies, as has happened in the real world countless times.)

Nozick also says very little about procedural fairness in the societies that grow into minimal states. What he does say, however, implies that he believes unanimity to be the only legitimate decision procedure. So if a minimal state were to have citizen participation in its decision-making processes, then it would have to be in terms of unanimous agreement, and this, of course, completely lacks practicality, or connection to the real world, given that large groups of individuals hardly ever can agree unanimously concerning important matters.[3]

---

[3]It was disconcerting to read through a theoretical tract of over three hundred pages dealing with the nature of a just state and find not one significant reference to elections, representative government, or decision procedures for the enactment of society-wide rules. Nozick says that individuals in a state of nature would join together into protective associations but says nothing about their having a voice in the decision-making processes of their associations. He also doesn't say what they might do if dissatisfied with the way a dominant association is being run, except that they could go elsewhere for protection.

Notice, by the way, that Nozick cannot say that unanimity is required only at a meta-decision-level, when a minimal state selects fundamental governing rules, so that when deliberating on that level they might unanimously adopt a more practical everyday decision procedure. He cannot say this, for that would amount to an abandonment of the guts of his theory by legitimizing most of the measures he denies can be enacted by a morally upright state, including redistribution legislation that might be accepted by a majority of association members.

In any case, Nozick's argument against the legitimacy of a more-than-minimal state is defective in another way. Nozick envisions associations offering individuals protection from unjustified boundary crossings, contract violations, and the like, but there is nothing within his system that forbids associations from offering other services as well; indeed, he expects that they would. A protective association might become dominant precisely by offering health insurance, high-quality medical facilities, first-rate highways, schools, or even the convenience of charity management. Nozick provides no reasons for thinking that this would be any less likely than his own scenario or that it would be any more invasive of individual rights.

Another way to put the point is this: Nozick believes that individuals have the right to do whatever they wish with their wealth, including the right privately to redistribute it or to invest it in for-profit cooperative ventures (i.e., companies and corporations) of virtually any kinds that do not infringe on the natural rights of other individuals. It is protective associations, governments, and states that he says violate Lockean natural rights when they engage in these activities. But a protective association would be, in fact, a profit-making private enterprise offering services to those willing to buy them. What reason having to do with violations of Lockean natural rights would forbid them from offering the various kinds of services just mentioned in addition to the protective ones Nozick allows them to provide?

This brings us again to what is perhaps the underlying difficulty with Nozick's line of reasoning, namely, that it does not have much to do with the true human situation.[4] Human beings are essentially social animals whose inner psyches ache for a friendlier atmosphere than would be provided by minimal states restricted to "the narrow functions of protection against force, theft, fraud, enforcement of contracts, and so

---

[4]Sheldon Wolin forcefully makes this point in his excellent review of Nozick's book in *The New York Times* (May 11, 1974) Book Review section.

on," where the "and so on" does not include most of the sorts of things that all actual electorates have chosen (often by majority rule of elected representatives) to have their governments perform for them.

Finally, we need to consider Nozick's entitlement theory, the guts of his position concerning economic justice and the part of his theory that has received the lion's share of attention in journal articles and in the mass media. What he says is supposed to be part of, or to follow from, his Lockean starting points, and in a nutshell comes down to this: You can justly appropriate any unowned property, provided doing so does not worsen the situations of others in ways different from just depriving them of the opportunity to acquire that particular bit of property or from increasing competition in a commodity they sell—unless you adequately compensate those harmed so that their overall situation is not worsened. Once you own a commodity, you can do with it what you will, provided you don't violate the moral boundaries of others. No one, however, can justly purchase or be given property if that would provide them with a complete monopoly of the type of goods in question. Finally, in the event that goods are owned in ways that do not accord with all of the above, justice requires that these illicit holdings be distributed to those who, to the best of our ability to ascertain, would now justly have possession had the illicit transfers of goods not taken place.

Nozick's theory concerning just holdings and their transfer dovetails with mine in taking account of the competitive nature of the human animal. But in every other way, our theories are quite different (and *vive la différence!*).

He has a rather blockbuster conception of private ownership: owners can do whatever they want with their goods provided they don't invade the moral boundaries of others. Presumably, then, owners of priceless historical relics or anthropological artifacts cannot be prohibited from putting them to the torch if they so desire, and even in wartime, private property cannot legitimately be expropriated by the state. On my view, of course, a society may choose many other sorts of conventions concerning the ownership of property, including holding all property in common. It may, for example, force the sale of land to be used for highways, or forbid the construction of eyesores, without treating anyone unfairly.

In explaining my own theory, the problem of rectifying illicit property acquisitions that occurred long ago was not addressed, but clearly my theory does not require that this be done. In any case, Nozick's insistence that this sort of restitution be made, so far as it is possible to do so, is completely impractical. Would Nozick have us give the Western Hemisphere back to descendents of the Native Americans who originally owned it?

Finally, Nozick, unlike this writer, thinks of market forces as determining fair prices. That is the point of his famous Wilt Chamberlain example: if hundreds of thousands of basketball fans willingly pay Chamberlain twenty-five cents extra to see him play, then Nozick believes that Chamberlain has justly acquired the resulting small fortune.[5] Presumably, Nozick also believes the implication of all this, namely that, for example, when people are pressed to the wall by market forces beyond their control and thus are forced to work for starvation wages, the resulting exchanges of one kind of wealth (labor) for another (a pittance in wages) are fair. But perhaps what is at issue here is not philosophical but rather economic; perhaps Nozick doesn't believe that free markets ever put people into this kind of bind, except when due to their own errors or laziness. Perhaps he doesn't believe that, in general, economic power in a free marketplace favors the rich and/or well-placed. (One wonders what Nozick would say about those foolish enough to be born to poor parents at a time when all land and the rights to ordinary goods already have been appropriated. Perhaps he expects that they would create new wealth starting from scratch, without the benefit of public schools, highways, health benefits, or other governmental helping hands, or that, *a la* Horatio Alger, they would get lucky and have rich benefactors come to their aid. Anyway, as to those not sufficiently brilliant, or lucky, well, . . . perhaps Nozick would agree with the immortal words of one of today's college students: "It's a doggy dog world, isn't it?")

It should be clear, then, that Nozick's theory, while agreeing with mine in being contractual, is otherwise quite different, and that this writer finds little to applaud, and much that is wrongheaded, in Nozick's theory.

---

[5]The same principle would apply to textbook royalties, a consequence of Nozick's theory with which (hope springing eternally in the human breast) this textbook writer is unwilling to publicly dispute.

David Gauthier's Contract Theory

Page 4 (opening paragraph)

... [W]hatever force moral claims have derives ... entirely from their role in overcoming the structural problem of interaction represented by the Prisoner's Dilemma, the problem of reconciling individual maximizing action with Pareto-optimality. Anything else would only be a mythical addendum that ... would leave morality as impotent as religion.

—David Gauthier

David Gauthier's theory, as proposed in his extremely dense and academic-jargon-ridden book *Morals by Agreement,* and also in his replies to critics, is unusual in that he tries to generate a moral system from scratch, without appealing to any presystematic moral principles or sentiments whatsoever.[1]

According to Gauthier, rational agents will behave in a moral manner because it is in their long-term nonmorally motivated interests to do so. His position thus definitely is not the one, championed by this writer and many others, that rational agents try to maximize their overall interests, among which is an interest in being moral. Gauthier makes it clear that his intent is to generate moral obligations without appeal to prior moral items of any kind. But he doesn't claim that these rational constraints are identical with any particular ordinary moral code, say, of the kind "learned from parents, peers, priests and teachers."

---

[1]David Gauthier, *Morals by Agreement* (Oxford: Clarendon Press, 1986). He replied to some of his critics in "Morality, Rational Choice, and Semantic Representation: A Reply to My Critics," *Social Philosophy and Policy* 5 (Spring 1988) 173–221, and in "Why Contractarianism?" and in "Rational Constraint: Some Last Words," in *Contractarianism and Rational Choice: Essays on David Gauthier's* Morals by Agreement, ed. Peter Vallentyne (New York and Cambridge: Cambridge University Press, 1991). All quotations of Gauthier in this chapter are from *Morals by Agreement.*

Recall that in a prisoner's dilemma, the straightforward attempt by both parties to gain the maximum profit results in their both receiving a much lesser reward. Gauthier believes that in a perfect marketplace, choices would be neither morally right nor morally wrong because, unlike the case of a prisoner's dilemma, players could maximize their own benefits while still allowing all the other bargainers also to maximize their "utilities" (Gauthier loves game theory jargon).[2] But perfect markets rarely, if ever, exist, and so there is need for a moral principle that properly constrains behavior "when mutual benefit is not assured by the pursuit of individual gain." In iterated prisoner's dilemmas, the problem is solved when both parties assume a strategy something like tit-for-tat; in nonperfect marketplaces, Gauthier says, rational bargainers equal in knowledge, economic strength, and the like, solve the similar problem by adopting his moral principle of rational cooperation.

His arguments are quite complicated, but the underlying idea is this: One might suppose that, in bargaining situations, enlightened self-interest would always direct us to choose *utility maximizing strategies.* Gauthier calls those who use this strategy *straightforward maximizers.* In fact, Gauthier notes, self-interest does so when maximizing utilities in this way is *optimal,* which means that "there is no possible outcome affording some person a greater utility and no person a lesser utility." Presumably, in perfect marketplaces, strategies always are available that are both utility maximizing for all parties, thus producing outcomes that are in "equilibrium," and also optimizing. But in imperfect marketplaces, this is not always the case, and that is why morality enters the picture: . . . [M]oral theory is essentially the theory of optimizing constraints on utility-maximization." Bargainers who are roughly equal in intelligence and knowledge; who have "perfect information about possible actions, possible outcomes, and all preferences over these outcomes"; and who bargain under certain other conditions (some of which will be mentioned shortly) cannot maximize their benefits by demanding more than an amount that is optimal, and that is why rationality sometimes restricts utility maximization choices by means of a "meta

---

[2]Roughly speaking, a perfect marketplace is one in which (1) each of the more or less equally intelligent players knows what every other player will do and knows the outcome of each possible action; (2) all goods are privately owned; (3) the use or consumption of goods by one person precludes their use or consumption by others; (4) no one can gain by the losses of others nor does anyone care about the welfare of others; and (5) the production, exchange, or consumption of relevant property does not affect the "utility" of unrelated parties.

choice, a choice about how to make choices." Gauthier calls those who bargain in this way *constrained maximizers.*

The principle of rational cooperation Gauthier specifies is that of *minimax relative concession,* a game theory principle that is "a measure of each person's stake in a bargain—the difference between the least he might accept in place of no agreement, and the most he might receive in place of being excluded by others from agreement." Acting morally, for Gauthier, means coming to agreements with one's equals via the principle of minimax relative concession and carrying out those agreements when the other parties to them can be expected to do so.

But why should rational bargainers be constrained, rather than straight-forward, maximizers? Put into plain English, his answer (on which most of what he says in the latter part of his book, most of which will not be discussed here, depends) is this: When someone bargains in an imperfect marketplace with others who are equal in intelligence, knowledge, and so on, that person cannot gain the whole, or even the lion's share, of the profits of the cooperative venture, because other equal bargainers will not agree to a deal of this kind. Of course, if one bargainer is more knowledgeable than the others, or in some other way significantly superior to them, then that person might be able to gain a greater-than-equal share, but this is not possible with *equal* bargainers (presumably because, being equal, they all have equal leverage). The principle of minimax relative concession instructs bargainers who are more or less equal in the ways Gauthier has specified to accept as much as they can get under the circumstance, which he believes means settling for the same share every other partner to the deal settles for. Thus, in a two person case, each person will settle for half of the profits (omitting complexities that need not concern us here). And this is what his principle of minimax relative concession counsels.

An obvious sticking point in Gauthier's theory, as he states it early in his book, is that he has his equal rational agents be "transparent," which means that they know whether other bargainers will or won't comply with agreements made by means of minimax relative concessions. He later agrees that this is too unrealistic and appeals instead to "a more realistic *translucency,* so that their dispositions to co-operate or not may be ascertained by others, not with certainty, but as more than mere guesswork," and then presents a long argument to show that constrained maximizers who develop their ability to detect cheaters will benefit from becoming adept at this skill more than will straightforward maximizers.

Fortunately, we need not go into his extremely involved attempt to prove this, except to note, first, that his proof deals only with bargaining situations that constitute prisoner's dilemmas; and second, that it depends on the way in which he assigns values to the four possible outcomes when a bargain has been struck. The values he specifies are one, assigned to defection when the other party cooperates; zero, assigned to cooperation when the other party defects; two-thirds, to mutual cooperation; and one-third, to mutual defection. We also should mention his supposition that the population of the bargainers he deals with evenly divides between constrained and straightforward maximizers.

To succeed in his attempt to derive a moral standard from strictly nonmoral elements, Gauthier has to prove three things: first, that agents equal in the relevant ways maximize their profits (given the demands of other bargainers) via minimax relative concessions; second, that when agreements have been made in this way, rational agents will keep them; and third, that by identifying morally right choices with his principle of rational cooperation, he has generated a satisfactory moral system starting from nonmoral premises. In this writer's opinion, Gauthier's attempt fails on all three counts.

Perhaps the principal reason for believing that Gauthier has not constructed a satisfactory moral system is that he has morality enter into the picture only in the rarest sorts of circumstances, namely, when rational agents bargain who are equal in all the ways described earlier (and even then only when a few other circumstances obtain). It thus renders morality of next to no consequence in the great sweep of things. This is perhaps the most frequently raised objection to Gauthier's theory. (Gilbert Harmon, for instance, nicely makes this point in an article that is very critical of Gauthier's theory.[3])

However, even in the exceedingly rare cases in which he sees moral considerations as being relevant, his minimax principle of rational cooperation yields results most of us, certainly this writer, would find intuitively far off the mark. His McGee/Grasp example illustrates this nicely. Sam McGee discovers the richest vein of gold in the Yukon but lacks the one hundred dollars needed to register his claim. According to Gauthier, "If Grasp, the banker, is the only man in Dawson City with the ready cash to lend to McGee, then poor Sam will (rationally) have to offer Grasp a half-share in the claim. For although Grasp's $100 is

---

[3]Gilbert Harmon, "Rationality in Agreement: A Commentary on Gauthier's *Morals by Agreement,*" *Social Philosophy and Policy* 5 (Spring 1988): 1–16.

worth only $100 in the absence of McGee's discovery, yet McGee's discovery is worthless to him without Grasp's money." Indeed, Gauthier has to say that a fifty-fifty split is the correct division of profits no matter how much money the lender supplies, whether ten dollars or ten million dollars, or how much profit will be gleaned from McGee's mine. Although Gauthier says that "if a fair or impartial distribution of the cooperative surplus relates the benefit each person receives to the contribution he makes, each person's fair share of the surplus is determined by shares proportional to claims," this does not mean he agrees with my principle for fairly dividing profits. In two-person situations, Gauthier's theory requires that fair share (again omitting certain complexities) always is one-half: "In affording equal or equivalent shares of the co-operative surplus to all persons, the principle of minimax relative concession ensures that bargaining impartially relates each person's contribution to co-operation to the benefit he receives from it." Very few who write concerning moral theory, certainly not this writer, will agree with Gauthier on this point.

What Gauthier has to say about McGee and Grasp, by the way, illustrates how extremely unusual cases have to be for Gauthier to believe that moral considerations apply. Immediately after his remark about McGee's discovery being worthless without Grasp's money, Gauthier says: "Of course, if there are other sources of funds, Sam is in a position comparable to Ms Macquarrie [who need not pay an employee half of her profits because there are other people available to do the employee's job]; he needs money but not Grasp's money, so he can borrow at the going rate. But in the Dawson City of our example there is, alas, no going rate [and thus McGee has to share profits equally with Grasp]." The implication is that moral considerations do not apply when one party is more needy than the other, so that the less needy bargainer can take the lion's share of profits without violating any moral strictures. In most real life cases, of course, there are many sources of borrowed funds, and thus, according to Gauthier's theory, moral considerations are not relevant.

Note, by the way, that strictly speaking, the McGee/Grasp bargaining situation does not constitute a true prisoner's dilemma. So if Gauthier intends his principle of rational cooperation to enter into the picture only in order to solve prisoner's dilemmas, then it surely does not apply in this case (nor, indeed, in most, if not all, of the other cases he discusses). One of the many reasons it doesn't constitute a prisoner's dilemma is that McGee can defect after Grasp has cooperated whereas

Grasp cannot defect after McGee has cooperated. (In fairness to Gauthier, however, it needs to be said that most of his examples do bear some sort of resemblance to genuine prisoner's dilemmas, or at least to one of the other, similar dilemmas discussed in chapter 18.)

In spite of Gauthier's exceedingly complicated arguments to prove the rationality of making agreements via his minimax principle, it clearly frequently is not rational to do so. In the example at hand, for instance, it would seem to be rational for Grasp, being less needy than McGee, to take advantage of McGee's desperate need for cash and demand much more than half of the profits. Moreover, in some other kinds of cases, it might well be sensible for one of the bargainers to make a deal affording them less than half of the profits, for instance in order to gain a larger volume of business (a point made by Gilbert Harmon in his recently footnoted article).

Gauthier's proof that constrained maximization is a better strategy than is straightforward maximization also is defective because it deals only with bargainers who are translucent. In real life, we often get stabbed in the back by people we have judged to be trustworthy. Flesh-and-blood human beings all too often are not translucent, the reason for the remark early in this work that one of life's chief problems is trying to determine who can, and who cannot, be trusted.

Anyway, even if it would be rational for Gauthier's equal agents to come to agreements in the way Gauthier specifies, it frequently would be in their narrow interests to violate them. Gauthier's proof that it would always be in their interest to comply is not adequate. For one thing, his reasoning only concerns bargaining situations that, unlike most real-life cases, constitute prisoner's dilemmas. For another, he provides no justification whatsoever for assigning the values that he does to the four possible outcomes (defection/cooperation, mutual cooperation, mutual defection, and cooperation/defection), or for assuming that there are an equal number of constrained and straightforward maximizers. The latter assumption, in particular, is dubious. In everyday life, defectors, especially those who cleverly cultivate a reputation for honesty, often profit immensely at the expense of fleeced cooperators taken in by their pose of honesty. In the real world, alas, defection often pays much better than cooperation, especially in single-case bargaining situations.

Finally, Gauthier's theory is intended to provide a moral standard for all sorts of interactions between equals, including those between spouses, and even between whole peoples. But when interactions occur between unequals, he believes that morality does not apply and that rational agents will straightforwardly maximize their own nonmoral interests. The result is that his theory does not label immoral husbands who throw over wives for younger women (to mention just one of the more common moral crimes committed these days), and condones even the most heinous sorts of behavior that almost every other well-known theory would label grossly immoral.

Here, for example, is what Gauthier has to say about the Spanish subjugation of native populations in the Americas:

> "We may say that those possessing a superior technology are more rational than their fellows, in being better able to relate and devise means to their ends. . . . Our argument . . . rests on an assumption of equal rationality among persons which differences in technology deny. . . . In reconciling reason and morals, we do not claim that it is never rational for one person to take advantage of another. . . . We do claim that justice, the disposition not to take advantage of one's fellows, is the virtue appropriate to co-operation, voluntarily accepted by equally rational persons. Morals arise in and from the rational agreements of equals." (pp. 231–232)

In another place, he says, "Among unequals, one party may benefit most by coercing the other, and on our theory would have no reason to refrain."

These passages put into sharp focus the major difference between Gauthier's theory and mine (not to mention the vast majority of other theories proposed in the past several thousand years). We both approach the problem of moral right and wrong from the point of view of rational decision theory; we both see moral theory as subjectively grounded; and both of our theories are contractual in nature. But his theory, definitely unlike mine, judges the making and keeping of contracts morally compelling only in extremely few situations concerning agents he considers to be equals. As for the vast majority of cases arising in everyday life in which unequals interact, including the subjugation and murder of whole peoples, anything goes, morally speaking. In my opinion, of course, as in the opinions of most writers on the topic, relative lack of intelligence, economic strength, knowledge, or other capabilities does not make an individual fair game for unprincipled operators; technological superiority does not justify brutal aggression or mass murder.

In the Woody Allen film *Crimes and Misdemeanors,* one of the characters has his former lover murdered when she threatens to expose their affair to his wife. At first, he suffers remorse (for moral reasons having nothing to do with maximizing nonmoral utility!) that, if continued indefinitely, would prove his behavior less than optimal, but by the movie's end, he has overcome his remorse, as some do in real life, and cheerfully anticipates happily married bliss ever after. It is a clear implication of Gauthier's theory that a philanderer in the position of Allen's character would act rationally, and not immorally, by having his former lover cold-bloodedly murdered. Could a philosopher really intend this to be a consequence of his *moral* theory? Anyone who has doubts about Gauthier's intent should reflect on the fact that when asked at a private gathering whether his theory condoned what Woody Allen's nasty, grossly immoral character had done, Gauthier's response was that he would "bite the bullet."

23

More Recent Libertarian Theories

Practically everything done by modern governments violates someone or other's rights; and . . . practically everything they do is inefficient.

—Jan Narveson

The worker desires to get as much as possible, the master to give as little as possible. It is not, however, difficult to foresee which of the two parties must upon all ordinary occasions, have the advantage in the dispute.

—Adam Smith

Robert Nozick's 1974 award-winning book revived sagging interest in libertarian ideas about moral right and wrong, and with the 1986 appearance of David Gauthier's work, philosophical libertarianism moved into full swing. But in this writer's opinion, the underlying problems (of the kind discussed in the previous two chapters) that plague the theories of Nozick and Gauthier remain unresolved.

One of the serious problems with Nozick's theory, for example, is that he does not justify its Lockean natural rights underpinnings. Tibor Machan, in his book *Individuals and Their Rights,* attempts to fill this gap.[1] But he does so by means of a somewhat Aristotelian idea about how items are to be classified by means of genus/species definitions that reveal their essences (he prefers the term "natures"), an idea very few philosophers these days would be willing to accept. He says that human beings, to take the relevant example, are animals whose "difference"

---

[1]Tibor Machan, *Individuals and Their Rights* (LaSalle, Illinois: Open Court Publishing Company, 1989). All quotations of Machan in this chapter are from *Individuals and Their Rights.*

(Machan actually uses this Aristotelian term) from other animals—being rational and (following from this?) able to freely choose actions—reveals their fundamental nature.

The main features of his argument are these: (1) because we are by nature rational animals, we have a responsibility to best pursue our own development; (2) because we have free will, this responsibility is moral; (3) we have a natural right to whatever is required for our own development; (4) but having a social life that grants us this right obliges us to grant a similar right to others; (5) the Lockean rights to life, liberty, and property are implied by the right stated in (3) above; and (6) these rights justify a free-market economy and rule against socialistic systems.

The trouble with Machan's starting point is not simply that Aristotle's ideas about essences and genus/species definitions are out of fashion. It is, rather, among other things, that there is no single item such as rationality which distinguishes the human from the nonhuman animal realm. Not all human beings are rational, none are always rational, and we all are different from other animals in a great many other ways. In addition, it is clear now that if, say, four-footed, one-eyed rational creatures were discovered on another planet, they would not qualify as *Homo sapiens*. Machan says that in such an eventuality, we would have to change our definition. But this only shows that being rational cannot be the only way, or even the only relevant or essential way, in which we differ from other animals. It is just as important to an understanding of what it is to be human to see us as sexual creatures, social (pack) animals, superstitious (irrational) beings, as well as (sometimes) rational animals, disposed to favor close kin, frequently tempted to immorality, creators of religions, and so on, as it is to notice that we are rational and have free wills.

Even supposing, however, that being rational free agents correctly differentiated us from other animals, nothing pertaining to morality would follow from this, unless a moral element were already part of the conception of a freely choosing rational agent. (We cannot draw rabbits out of philosophical hats unless they are already in there.) But the ordinary conceptions of the relevant terms do not contain anything having to do with morality. We often, for example, freely choose a rational course of action that has no moral aspect to it whatsoever. (It is true, of course, that being free and rational is generally thought to be a necessary condition for being held morally responsible, but it isn't a sufficient one.)

Although Machan is somewhat unclear at this crucial point in his theory, he apparently intends to bridge the gap here between *is* and *ought* by the postulation of objective "human goods"—those items of value in fulfilling our development as human beings—which he then ties to moral goodness. For example, he says, "The *morally* good . . . is that aspect of the human good . . . open to choice." But even supposing that there are such things as objective human goods, it doesn't follow that those open to choice are morally good. Virtually all human goods are open to choice, but most choices (for example, to listen to a Bach Brandenburg concerto rather than a Mozart sonata, or to replace old plumbing rather than an old stove) are not generally seen as morally right or wrong.

To put the matter another way, Machan's claim that human goods open to choice are moral is false (although, of course, some of these goods are), but can be made true by employing a nonstandard conception of moral goodness from which this claim then will follow. My suspicion is that when moving from the merely human good to the morally good, Machan has indeed conceived of the morally good in a novel way that justifies this move, but that, without realizing it, in other places he reverts to a more usual conception from which his claim does not follow, thus becoming unintentionally guilty of equivocation.

It is difficult in general to know when, or even if, someone commits this kind of error. It may be that Machan has unintentionally equivocated on the concept of responsibility rather than, or perhaps in addition to, that of the morally good. Or it may be that, without realizing it, he has moved from the usual sense of responsibility, according to which we are responsible for our own development and have no one else to blame for our failures, to the somewhat different sense of *moral* responsibility, according to which we are accountable to others for certain kinds of choices. We can say, for example, that we are responsible for deciding whether to vacation in the mountains rather than at the sea, but this isn't a moral responsibility in the way, for instance, that someone who commits murder is said to be morally responsible. We cannot be certain as to what Machan has done here. Indeed, his error may not be in how he conceives of moral goodness, or of moral responsibility, but rather in conceiving at the crucial spot in his theory of all *choices* as moral choices. In any case, Machan has not justified his claim about the morally good being an aspect of human good open to choice, even supposing the concept of an objective human good makes sense.

If, as we've just argued, the first two of the six major features of Machan's theory fail to fly (as does the third feature, and for similar reasons), those remaining, and thus the rest of his theory, which depends on the first two, go down with them. But perhaps a comment on one additional feature of his system is in order here. Opponents often claim that libertarians fail to justify their claims about the virtues of free markets and the evils of governmental endeavors. Machan argues for free markets, in large part, by defending the right to own property. He argues that without private ownership we cannot delineate "the sphere of jurisdiction of each person's moral authority, where her own judgment is decisive"; that private ownership allows for the fullest possible realm of personal authority for all persons; and that "one (not others) ought to be the authority over items or processes one has recognized and made valuable or received from someone, or from a series of persons who have done the same."

Space considerations preclude a detailed discussion of this argument, but note three things. First, the problem of specifying moral rights seems to be no more difficult for people who live in societies where there are few, or even no, privately held items than for those who live in groups where most goods are privately owned. There are all too many alternatives in either case. Second, although true that individuals have little say concerning the use of publicly held goods, they also have little say concerning the use of goods privately held by others. So it cannot be said ahead of time and in general which kind of system maximizes personal authority.[2] (More will be said about this point shortly.) Third, Machan's Nozick-like principle concerning just holdings does not follow from his starting point in human nature.

As we have just seen, Tibor Machan argues for his libertarian theory by means of metaphysical ideas about definitions and essences. Jan Narveson, in his book *The Libertarian Idea,* explicitly eschews metaphysical arguments about essences (he also writes in a clear manner which contrasts rather strikingly with Machan's more murky style).[3] Narveson wants to see how well he can defend libertarian theory, and like Gauthier, he wants to do so without appeal to moral "intuitions." However, unlike Gauthier, he is concerned primarily with social issues.

---

[2] Most economists, and this writer, contend that systems of the kind Machan envisions (as do Nozick and most libertarians), in which, for instance, some children inherit great wealth and its competitive advantages, are bound to provide greater "realms of personal authority" to the wealthy than to the poor, thus not satisfying Machan's own requirement (and in my terms making them competitively unfair to those with fewer opportunities).

[3] Jan Narveson, *The Libertarian Idea* (Philadelphia: Temple University Press, 1988). All quotations of Narveson in this chapter are from *The Libertarian Idea.*

He wants to generate "moral principles for societies out of the nonmoral values of individuals."

But Narveson's defense of libertarianism is not dogmatic; his intent is to defend libertarianism to the extent that it can be defended, in particular by seeing how well it might work in the real world, but he is not loath to consider counterexamples. His conclusion is that libertarian systems would work rather well, although he does note at least two exceptions and, as we shall see, his investigation lends better support to a somewhat more modest idea than to a strictly libertarian position. He borrows a great deal from Gauthier, including arguments about constrained maximizers, pareto-efficiency, and solutions to prisoner's dilemmas.

The moral principle he attempts to defend, which he thinks would be agreed to by hypothetical agents in a state of nature, is that "our sole basic duty is to refrain from utilizing the fundamental resources of others without their consent, and those resources include, at a minimum, the bodies and minds of those others." The implications of this idea, he says, require, at a minimum, the following:

> "(1) We have no *fundamental* general duty to provide others with such goods [even] as the necessities of life; (2) we have a general duty not to interfere with . . . [a truly free] market; (3) we should always in general prefer voluntary social arrangements to involuntary ones whenever . . . feasible. (4) Governments . . . are severely restricted in what they may properly do, and the blessings of a majority vote in favor of a given government activity is not in general a sufficient license of that activity, morally speaking." (p. 165)

This agreement, he says, is libertarian in maximizing the role of private efforts while minimizing that of governments.

The chief problem encountered by egoistically inclined moral theorists is to justify the move from personal self-interest to a moral standard. Narveson does this by employing the notion of contractually generated obligation. He sees a person's best interests as being served by agreements to cooperate with others rather than fight. We need the assurance that others will not trample on us, and we can attain it only by granting them the same assurance: "The concern we must by nature have with our own values . . . is such as to underwrite a social principle allowing each to pursue that person's possibly very different ones."

Although it is very likely true that in certain kinds of situations rational agents all do better by agreeing, and even by conforming, to such a principle rather than by fighting, one can imagine others in which some might do even better in other ways. They might do better, for instance, by forming alliances that "take over" the governance of every-one in a given area, thereby forming a ruling aristocracy much on the order of innumerable actual cases. But supposing that self-interested rational agents did agree to cooperate on the conditions Narveson spec-ifies, why wouldn't they "defect" when it suited their purposes? Narve-son's answer is taken pretty much from Gauthier's arguments con-cerning the superiority of cultivating the disposition to constrained, rather than to straightforward, maximization (he even discusses the matter in terms of prisoner's dilemmas), an answer that, as mentioned in chapter 22, is defective at least in neglecting more subtle strategies that are the stock-in-trade of scoundrels.

Anyway, there are all sorts of other contracts (Rawls's, for one). Why would any of us select Narveson's contract? His answer, roughly speaking, is that it is the best deal we can get for ourselves. Although we would do better with a contract that improved our own situation by harming those of others, we can't expect these others to agree to it. But why does a contract that so severely limits the actions of governments maximize self-interest best? His answer, roughly speaking, is two-fold.

The first part is his claim that virtually everything governments do violates someone or other's rights. But this is question begging if, as Narveson insists, it is contracts that generate moral obligations and rights—remember that he eschews appeals to subjective moral senti-ments (intuitions) or to objective natural rights.[4]

It might be argued, of course, that rational agents would prefer as much freedom of action as possible and so would rather agree to a gov-ernment that restricted their liberties the least than to a more restrictive or coercive one. But, as remarked when discussing Machan's theory, we cannot say ahead of time, or in general, whether private or public enterprises restrict or coerce behavior the most.

Notice, by the way, that Narveson's principal argument against having governments run by majority rule—that this amounts to the use of force against those who vote nay—never seriously takes account of the possi-bility of unanimous meta-agreements to abide by certain majority deci-sions, or of the impracticality of having even the tiniest minimal govern-ments function by unanimous decision. It also passes over the fact that private corporations, at least in theory, also generally are overseen by less-than-unanimous stockholder agreements and that all citizens have at

---

[4]Governments, of course, often violate their own laws, but then private enterprises of-ten violate their own contracts.

least a tiny say in all government-run institutions but none in completely private (nonstock) organizations we may be forced by monopolies or cartels to rely on.

The second reason that Narveson provides for his belief that self-interest is maximized by agreeing to a contract that severely limits the actions of governments is his claim that governments almost always are less efficient than private enterprises. (Many hold that efficiency, unlike rights violations, is not a moral concern. Narveson thinks that the two blend into each other, partly on grounds relating to pareto-efficiency, but let's pass over this issue here.) Most of the last half of his book is taken up with an attempt to see how far this claim can be defended by examining particular cases. We can't go into every, or even most, of the details he considers, but perhaps a few comments will suggest why this writer finds his defense unsuccessful and often more supportive of a different idea, indeed one that Narveson himself sometimes seems to endorse.

His arguments and examples often exhibit a naivete as to how the real world functions. Consider, for example, the way he describes the distinction between artificial monopolies, created by government rules forbidding competition, and natural ones "where some private enterprise, by virtue of superior products, more efficient operation, fortunate situation in relation to supply sources, or lassitude on the part of potential competitors, ends up with all the business, even though no one has been forcibly [by government] prevented from entering the market." Overlooked are the more usual methods by which monopolies are formed, such as the strong arm tactics employed by Standard Oil in the late nineteenth century or the formation of cartels that corner the market on a product so as to jack up the price.

His arguments concerning discrimination on the basis of race, or sex, in hiring provide another example. He points out that sometimes these are relevant to the job. For example, a model for women's underwear should be a woman; the minister of a Black Muslim church someone who is black. He also points out that requiring employers to pay the same wages for women as for men removes a market incentive to employ women. But he passes over the devastating effects discrimination can have on those discriminated against, effects that are inefficient for them obviously, but also are for others in society who must bear increased police and other costs. (He also neglects the ways in which discrimination violates moral sentiments concerning fair play, but that is deliberate on his part; he doesn't want to appeal to moral sentiments.)

Some of Narveson's other arguments, if not naive, at least depend on extremely optimistic estimates, in particular of the altruistic tendencies of most human beings. Concerning the education of children, for instance, he argues that "a very small fraction of the populace [at most 15 percent] would in fact be seriously unable to finance their children's education" and, as to who would pay for this 15 percent, he lists those "sincerely desiring that these children get an education; . . . firms . . . that might be able to utilize their services . . . ; people who fear the consequences of children who go without education . . . ; [and] schools themselves . . . as many private schools do even now." His argument thus rests on an overgenerous appraisal of the ways in which corporate needs will solve this social problem and of the extent of human kindness or concern for others.[5]

Some of the other Narveson arguments and claims are rather simplistic (if not downright false). One example that rankled this writer a great deal was Narveson's remark that "Studies have confirmed what common sense and Aristotle have both told us for a couple of millennia: if a child is properly brought up, it will have the disposition to cooperate and to obey reasonable rules. And if it is not, then it very likely won't."

Moreover, Narveson often argues for one aspect of his theory, say liberty, while neglecting another, say efficiency, thus passing over what may be the most relevant examples. For instance, he argues against having the state require sellers to provide product information free of charge on the ground that it is in the interests of sellers to impart "enough information to the consumer to induce him to buy" anyway. He also argues that consumers are not entitled to this free information so that a seller is "enslaved if we require him . . . to supply it." These arguments, however, neglect, first, the fact that the cost of supplying the information inevitably gets passed on to consumers, so that they don't get something for nothing; second, that sellers frequently have not supplied relevant information until required to by law; third, that a different sort of social contract might not make this requirement into a kind of slavery; and fourth, that it is more *efficient* to have sellers provide the information rather than to have consumers ferret it out if they can (think only of the recent food labeling laws that provide consumers with important information not provided prior to these laws). Narveson's point that pri-

---

[5]When opponents argue that free markets will fail, Narveson frequently sees private charity as the savior, thus implying that free markets sometimes *do* fail, and also neglecting the cumulative effect on those who are charitable in their competitions with others who in this way are free riders.

vate enterprises could (do? would?) supply this information for a fee neglects the higher costs this would entail to consumers, particularly in time. Think of how much more convenient, and cheaper, it is to have producers, best able to gather the information, provide it at the point of purchase.

To his credit, Narveson often does see arguments on the other side of an issue, and to some extent does alter his overall position about the superior efficiency and overall desirability of market as compared to state actions, but usually in the end he still touts free markets. He notes, for instance, that the government-run health plan in Ontario, Canada, where he lives, has lower overhead costs than private plans in the United States and that "a great many people are manifestly happier with that medical system, and nobody is worse off," thus even perhaps making the Ontario plan pareto-efficient. He then concludes with the "moral that a doctrinaire rejection of public systems in favor of private ones is not *automatically* forthcoming even if one shares libertarian sympathies. Facts really do matter!" The implication of this, and other remarks elsewhere, supports the much more plausible (nonlibertarian) idea that we should let private enterprises do what they do better than governments and, as in the case of Ontario's health system, have governments do those things they do better than private organizations. Yet, later on, he implies that he has made a better case for libertarianism than his own arguments would indicate.

His discussion of highways contains this same kind of ambivalence. He points to restrictions against traveling in large areas of the then Soviet Union as evidence that public ownership does not guarantee access even to publicly owned property (dubious as an example), and suggests ways in which private ownership might be consistent with needed access to property. But he also mentions problems with private ownership of highways and discusses how possible solutions might anyway make them run very much like publicly owned ones, although the success of private enterprise even at doing this would be somewhat problematic.[6] Yet, in the end, he says that user-cooperatives and private corporation ownership "make a good deal of sense, and a great deal more sense than putting [highways] in the hands of the police [the state]."

---

[6] "When privatization is proposed as an alternative, there looms before us the vision of what amounts to national borders every couple of hundred yards, or every few miles at most." Possible solutions such as coordinated toll booths or better payment when buying gas get close to looking "very like a tax on gasoline" and, anyway, how would "it differ, details apart, from what we actually have [with public ownership]?"

Narveson's discussion of highways also illustrates how he often neglects fairly obvious counterexamples to his claims about private ownership. He says next to nothing about, for example, ways in which governments protect those who use highways by requiring motorists to drive with care, not drive under the influence, pass tests to obtain driving licenses, and obtain insurance at least against damage to other parties. And he doesn't take seriously the monopolistic opportunities to jack up the price of highway use that might very well make travel much more expensive and thus less efficient, not to mention therefore tending to inhibit the liberty to travel.

Furthermore, Narveson doesn't discuss several vital activities that are better performed by governments, or by being forced on private enterprise by governments. Perhaps the chief threat to human existence in these post-cold-war days is the one posed by viruses, bacteria, and fungi. New viral strains coming out of Africa, for example, pose an especially serious threat of a kind that has never existed before. On the bright side, cheap nuclear fusion power looms on the horizon, but its development privately, if it ever succeeded, would be bound to take much longer than government-aided development. Anyway, even if successful, private development might well provide monopolistic opportunities for immense profits that limit the freedom and opportunity of others. Surely these are areas in which prudence, efficiency, and every other sort of reason rule against libertarian insistence that private always is better than public.

Finally, in this writer's opinion, the principal flaws in Narveson's theory, as in Nozick's and Gauthier's, result from his attempt to derive moral principles starting from self-interested, nonmoral considerations. He thus fails to take into account the moral sentiments that might be used to support arguments about what sorts of social contracts rational (and also moral!) agents might agree to. For the same reason, he fails in his arguments as to why his rational agents would conform to agreements once made (fails because it often is moral sentiments that, in fact, keep rational individuals from straying). But even those libertarians who might want to take account of moral sentiments when constructing their systems would, in this writer's opinion, also fail, because of the dubious nature of the claims they must make concerning the higher moral nature, or at least the greater efficiency, of private as compared to governmental activities.

When reading John Rawls, one is struck with how mindful he is of what life is like in the real world. When reading most libertarian tracts, the impression is one of divorce from reality resulting from their carrying too far the quite sensible, and extremely important, idea that governments can be, and often are, seriously inefficient and (to different extents in different societies) unfair and oppressive. Libertarians fail to consider the likelihood that the problem is not government, for which the solution is free enterprise, but rather the nature of human nature that has evolved over countless centuries. When constructing social, political, or economic systems, theorists need to take account of what science tells us about this evolutionary process and its end product—us—and at least take account of the vital fact that *human beings are in-group/out-group social animals moved by moral and other-regarding sentiments and, at the same time, by sentiments of an often contrary selfish nature.*

24

Meritarian versus Egalitarian Principles

An imbalance between rich and poor is the oldest and most fatal
ailment of republics.

— Plutarch

When the plowman plows, and the thresher threshes, they ought to
do so in the hope of sharing in the harvest.

— 1 Corinthians 9:10

From each according to his ability; to each according to his need.

— Karl Marx

From each according to his ability; to each according to his work.

— Joseph Stalin

Share and share alike.

— Old saying

Anyone who comes to hold a particular position in philosophy is bound
to wonder why so many others hold a contrary view. In my own case,
the relevant contrary view here is egalitarianism, a theory held by several of my close philosopher friends, not to mention (at least to some
extent) John Rawls and other well-known writers. Rawls's ideas on the
question of meritarian versus egalitarian standards are of particular interest to me because he does not defend his opinion by appeal either to
objective nonmoral facts or to "metaphysical" arguments. The implication of his overall theory is that his acceptance of a somewhat egalitarian principle is based on subjective moral sentiments. Why then his disagreement with this writer on this matter?

Earlier in this work, in particular in chapter 4, arguments were provided, based on evolutionary theory and an appeal to carefully considered sentiments, for supposing that meritarian principles are the dominant ones in the minds of most fair-minded individuals. Why, then, should egalitarianism have the appeal that it does? It seems to me that there are four likely explanations.

First, in at least two very important kinds of cases, feelings of affection, care, compassion, and the like, often overrule, or at least modify, meritarian sentiments concerning the distribution of goods. This is true without doubt among close kin, where, for instance, no matter how unable or unwilling some are to produce goods, all usually share in the basic necessities of life. (Children, of course, are not expected to produce in proportion to their consumption, but this is often true also of other family members.) It also is true, although to a lesser extent, among close friends. Meritarian sentiments evolved because we are genetic competitors. Close kin compete much less than unrelated individuals. Friends are seen as allies against others more than as genetic competitors.

The point is that it isn't easy to separate sentiments of one kind, motivating one kind of behavior, from sentiments of another, motivating a different kind of response. For example, we may be aware of egalitarian or kin-altrustic sentiments when sharing food with close kin, but not notice the contrary tug of meritarian feelings of fair play. (Interestingly, in cases where there is perceived competition within a family, as for example, between siblings for parental favor, meritarian fair play sentiments often dominate those of affection, care, etc.) There is a natural tendency in all of us to lump together in one category, labeled *moral,* other-regarding sentiments such as empathy, affection, and compassion along with those concerning fair play or justice. Indeed, in this writer's opinion, philosophers, including this one at an earlier date, frequently are guilty of this fusion of somewhat diverse elements.[1]

It also is true of human nature that we are more inclined to share with

---

[1]One of the claims made by John Rawls that can be seen as supporting his egalitarian position is somewhat different, but is not uncommon in philosophical writings. He notes that talents such as brains, strength, and the like, are inherited; we don't earn them by working hard, or in any other way. Whether we have these talents, or not, is thus just a matter of luck, a nonmoral consideration. So he sees the fruits of the applications of unusually excellent talents as not deserved, morally speaking. But, as remarked in chapter 20, and passing over Aristotle's ideas about the development of one's faculties over time, this seems to this writer to make Rawls guilty of a misunderstanding concerning issues involving free will and determinism.

other members of our own in-group than with those in out-groups who, after all, are doubly competitors (as noted in chapter two). When in foreign lands, for instance, most people are more willing to go out of their way to help compatriots than foreigners. Note also that part of the unwritten social contract requires certain kinds of cooperation on a non-quid-pro-quo basis.

Second, when thinking about distributive justice, it is easy to concentrate on material goods and to overlook meritarian sentiments with respect to nonmaterial, positional goods, goods that, like status and honor, are by their very nature in short supply, and that even most egalitarians might on reflection see best awarded according to merit. (Note, by the way, that Rawls's difference principle applies to material wealth, not to other sorts of goods.) More will be said about this point in a moment.

We also frequently overlook one of the most important kinds of material goods, namely, mates (indeed we generally are loath to think of mates in this way). We don't think that mates should be assigned according to an egalitarian principle (say by lottery), but rather that better competitors deserve the mates they attract, and one thing that makes a competitor better is the higher social standing or greater weaalth often gained by superior performance of one kind or another.

The point this time is that if we consider all sorts of goods and not merely the commodities traded in the marketplace, then the meritarian position becomes more compelling and the egalitarian less. Perhaps those who favor more egalitarian theories neglect this way in which merit is commonly thought to have its greater reward.

Third, societies frequently, one might say generally, provide at least three important goods more or less equally to all citizens, namely, protection from outside aggression, protection from internal crime, and medicinal benefits (note, for instance, the outrage felt by many in the United States today because of the large difference between the health care received by the rich or well placed as compared to that received by most who are poor). It is natural to see these benefits as being distributed according to an egalitarian principle. But it makes better sense, it seems to this writer, to see them as rewards not for the production of material goods but rather for being good citizens. Note, for instance, that punishment for crimes consists typically in inflicting harms that innocent citizens are guaranteed protection against.

There also, of course, are other common social services that seem to support egalitarian theory, including education and access to highways.

In many societies, these are provided on a modestly equal basis to most individuals. But the provision of some of these services is better explained by appeal to sentiments concerning fair play that require a level playing field (education being an example), or as granted for practical considerations (highways and education being examples). Efficiency is gained by having public highways; a better work force, more loyal citizens; and fairer competition, by public support for education.

Fourth, in capitalistic societies, particularly the United States, the few at the top of the economic pecking order gain much more wealth than meritarian principles of the kind championed in this work would allow, while the many at the bottom receive much less. One common reaction to this odious state of affairs is to be attracted to nonmeritarian principles instead of paying attention to the fact that meritarian distributive principles are not being adhered to. Some people apparently find it easier to conclude that those whose enterprises produce great profits therefore, according to meritarian principles, deserve the billions they reap, than to challenge the idea that marketplaces reward according to merit. (This happens to have been true somewhat in my own case in my less reflective, much younger days.)

Notice, by the way, that the first three of the explanations just given dovetail rather nicely with what evolution theory might suggest. The ingroups in which our ancestors lived during most of the grand sweep of human evolution must have been rather small and cohesive, in that way resembling the hunting-and-gathering societies that have existed in recent times, and in these societies, more or less even divisions of material goods predominate. This may seem to support the idea that egalitarian sentiments should be the predominant ones in most of our minds, and there is indeed something to this line of reasoning. But it neglects certain relevant considerations. In hunting-and-gathering societies today, as in the recent past, material goods have tended to be scarce, and the most important of them, food and water, hard to preserve in large quantities. In addition, there is little division of labor in most small hunting-and-gathering societies, and even in those that are primarily pastoral, there is little division of labor other than that between males and females (females typically do more of the gathering, males the hunting); obtaining material goods tends to be a group activity (so slackers find it hard to conceal their behavior); and differences in productivity are much smaller from person to person than in modern industrial societies. This suggests that in early human societies, meritarian and egalitarian divisions of the material fruits of common efforts were much more alike than in today's industrial cultures.

All of this suggests that when goods become more plentiful, when differences in occupation or performance become more pronounced, when in-group bloodlines become more varied, and so on, then meritarian sentiments can come to the fore. It is instructive that in at least a few of today's pre-agricultural societies, as for example, those in the Kalahari desert in southern Africa, once material goods become more plentiful, private property also becomes more common, equal sharing becomes less prevalent, and material wealth tends to differ from person to person. In modern societies, as in those most people have lived in for the past ten thousand years or so, material wealth has become great enough to be accumulated and so large differences in material wealth have become possible, and in these societies meritarian principles have come to predominate.

Note also that in smaller, cohesive, cultures, just as in modern industrial societies, those who produce more material wealth tend to receive more and better nonmaterial rewards than do others, particularly with respect to social standing, power, and most importantly from a genetic point of view, access to the best mates (shirkers, on the other hand, generally receive less). This is true also of those who perform better in warfare with surrounding groups (with cowards receiving less).

It also is clear that group cohesiveness is an important factor in the success of an in-group in competition with surrounding out-groups, and one way in which cohesiveness can be achieved is through a (usually unwritten) social contract that provides all with equal protection from outside aggression, internal crime, and ill health. As remarked before, this can be perceived as meritarian, not egalitarian, because these benefits can be thought of as being bought by good citizenship. But perhaps some see this as evidence supporting the egalitarian position.

Finally, remember that in days of old, people lived in very small societies and thus tended, much more than we do in today's large and diverse societies, to be closely related as kin. There thus was much less genetic competition within a group (the more important genetic competition being with surrounding out-groups) than is the case today. Relationships also were much more likely to be carried out on the basis of friendship. Other-regarding sentiments such as affection, empathy, and compassion thus tended to affect behavior much more strongly than they do today, and the influence of these sentiments can easily be confused with, and indeed be fused with, the influence of those concerning fair play. This counts as a theoretical reason for meritarian principles being stronger than those that are egalitarian, but it also suggests that there should be a (smaller) tug in the direction of egalitarian fair play in most of us.

If all cooperative interactions were between identical twins, or even between parents and siblings, competitive instincts and their meritarian support would be dimmed considerably by caring, other-regarding sentiments. The business world would run like a close-knit family in which everyone tends to be greatly concerned about everyone else. But in fact, unfortunately, the marketplaces of today's large cultures are not like that. Most interactions are with nonkin and, more and more often in large industrial societies, with nonfriends. Other-regarding sentiments are submerged by those of a meritarian nature. This is a claim, anyway, that follows from the central thesis of this book about cooperative and competitive principles of fair play.

25

Conclusion

I must obey the inscrutable exhortations of my soul.
—Calvin (of "Calvin & Hobbes," explaining
why he was looking for frogs)

Five fundamental ideas underpin the theory explained and defended in this work. The first is that there are no objective moral directives, no moral oughts or ought nots, built into the furniture of the universe. We cannot look "out there" and find morality written in the stars, or deduce moral oughts, *a la* Kant, from the nature of rationality itself. The fundamental ethical data, as Hume insisted, are internal sentiments, feelings, and desires. It is rational to act morally, when it is, because in doing so we maximize our own interests, including those peculiar ones commonly labeled *moral*. The extremely rare, abnormal individuals who lack these internal tugs on behavior (we call them sociopaths) have no reason to play the game straight when they can get away with not doing so. But for the rest of us, it is something within our own psyches, not some external command or feature of reality, that so often makes it rational for us to be loyal and to keep our word, even when every other internal force urges defection.

The second underlying idea is that immediate introspection, unguided by serious philosophical reflection and by knowledge gained from what others have learned about the human condition and human nature, is unlikely to yield thoughts that capture our strongest, most enduring sentiments. We are a notoriously self-deceiving animal, and anyway the relevant sentiments are not by any means easily sorted out.

The third underlying idea is that in trying to sort out the tangle of relevant moral sentiments, it is wise to appeal to scientific theories, in particular these days to the theories evolutionary biologists recently have proposed concerning reciprocal altruism, and to take seriously their implication that the moral side of human nature evolved because it enabled our distant ancestors to gain the tremendous advantages of cooperative, reciprocal behavior. One way to find out where we are now is to discover how and why we have gotten here. That is why in this work the two principles of fair play have been given the featured roles.

The fourth underlying idea is that we are each other's most serious genetic competitors and that, having evolved as an in-group/out-group animal, genetic success has depended on competitive success both within our own group and on the success of our group in competition with surrounding groups. And yet, because the benefits of cooperative behavior are so great, we must cooperate with each other even though we are each other's most serious genetic competitors.

Finally, the fifth underlying idea is that it is important to note the differences in the various kinds of sentiments and urges philosophers have often placed together in one category labeled *moral,* from which they have derived all sorts of moral obligations. Human beings are moved by essentially eight kinds of psychological items that are relevant to the moral side of human nature, items that need to be distinguished one from the other: (1) ideas about what makes cooperative and competitive activities fair; (2) sentiments favoring the keeping of fair bargains and fair competitions; (3) sentiments such as affection, empathy, and compassion, that indirectly motivate fair play; (4) a strong desire to strike back at those who betray our trust; (5) a desire for the welfare of close kin, in particular offspring; (6) sentiments such as affection (different from the affection felt towards nonkin) that indirectly motivate kin altruism; (7) a need to be part of a group to which we owe special loyalty; and (8) a tendency (often in conflict with other internal forces) to regard the customs and standards of one's in-group as superior to those of other groups. Whether we employ the label *moral* narrowly, as is done in this work, or more widely, is relatively unimportant. What counts is that we distinguish, as most moral theorists have not (an important exception being Allan Gibbard), the various tugs on human behavior in terms of the categories evolutionary biologists have proposed in recent years—that we make our moral theories take account of this way of looking at the human condition. Introspection may, or may not, be the final arbiter on moral matters. But introspection unguided by what science tells us about human nature and how it evolved, in particular unguided by scientific theories about how moral sentiments foster the cooperative behavior that has produced a cornucopia of human benefits, is unlikely to get at the heart of the matter.

One final comment. In my opinion, the fact that evolution has instilled in us sentiments that favor the making and keeping of fair bargains, along with feelings of compassion, affection, empathy, and loyalty, bodes well for the future of the human species. But that evolution also has given us sentiments of a more selfish nature bodes ill. The future of the human species may well hinge on whether the former or the latter hold sway over the next hundred years, during which time science and industry will change the world in ways now hard to imagine. Cooperation, having provided *Homo sapiens* with tremendous benefits over the centuries, now promises important victories in the ongoing battles against illness, pain, and untimely death. Whether we learn how better to fairly cooperate with each other or instead use our ever increasing power in unfair competitive activities that produce greater and greater destruction and misery, seems to this writer to constitute the most important and most interesting question concerning the future of the human species.

Selected Bibliography

Axelrod, Robert & W. D. Hamilton. *The Evolution of Cooperation*. New York: Basic Books, 1984.

Cederblom, Jerry. "The Retributive Liability Theory of Punishment." In *Public Affairs Quarterly* 9 (Winter 1995). (Forthcoming).

Chagnon, Napoleon A. 1979. "Mate Competition, Favoring Close Kin, and Village Fissioning Among the Yanomamo Indians." In *Evolutionary Biology and Human Social Behavior: An Anthropological Perspective,* ed. Napoleon A. Chagnon and William Irons. North Scituate, Mass.: Duxbury Press.

Darwin, Charles. *The Origin of Species*. 1859. Reprint, New York: Collier Books, 1962.

——— [1871] 1981. *The Descent of Man, and Selection in Relation to Sex*. Princeton: Princeton University Press.

Dawkins, Richard. 1976. *The Selfish Gene*. New York and Oxford: Oxford University Press.

——— 1982. *The Extended Phenotype*. Oxford and San Francisco: W. H. Freeman.

Ekman, Paul. 1992. *Telling Lies: Clues to Deceit in the Marketplace, Politics, and Marriage*. New York: W. W. Norton & Co.

Fishkin, James S. 1979. *Tyranny and Legitimacy: A Critique of Political Theories*. Baltimore: Johns Hopkins University Press.

Flood, Merrill M. 1952. "Some Experimental Games." In *Research Memorandum RM-789*. Santa Monica, Calif.: RAND Corp.

Frank, Robert H. 1988. *Passions Within Reason*. New York: W. W. Norton & Co.

Fried, Charles. 1981. *Contract as Promise: A Theory of Contractual Obligation*. Cambridge: Harvard University Press.

Gauthier, David. 1986. *Morals by Agreement*. Oxford and New York: Clarendon Press.

——— "Morality, Rational Choice, and Semantic Representation: A Reply to My Critics." *Social Philosophy & Policy* 5 (Spring 1988): 173–221.

Gibbard, Allan. 1982. "Human Evolution and the Sense of Justice." In *Social and Political Philosophy,* Midwest Studies in Philosophy VII, ed. Peter A. French, Theodore E. Uehling, Jr. and Howard K. Wettstein.

——— 1990. *Wise Choices and Apt Feelings*. Cambridge: Harvard University Press.

Hamilton, W. D. 1964. "The Genetical Theory of Social Behavior." *Journal of Theoretical Biology* 7:1–32.

Harmon, Gilbert. "Rationality in Agreement: A Commentary on Gauthier's *Morals by Agreement.*" *Social Philosophy & Policy* 5 (Spring 1988): 1–16.

Henberg, Marvin. 1990. *Retribution: Evil for Evil in Ethics, Law, and Literature.* Philadelphia: Temple University Press.

Hobbes, Thomas. [1651] 1957. *Leviathan.* Oxford: Oxford University Press.

Kahane, Howard. 1980. "Making the World Safe for Reciprocity." In *Reason and Responsibility,* 5th ed. 1980, 8th ed. 1993, ed. Joel Feinberg, 479–486. Belmont, Calif.: Wadsworth Publishing Co.

——— 1993. "Sociobiology, Egoism, and Reciprocity." In *Moral Philosophy,* ed. Louis Pojman, 68–84. Indianapolis: Hackett Publishing Co.

Locke, John. [1706] 1979. *An Essay Concerning Human Understanding.* Oxford: Clarendon Press.

Machan, Tibor. 1989. *Individuals and Their Rights.* La Salle, Ill.: Open Court Publishing Co.

Mackie, J. L. 1977. *Ethics: Inventing Right and Wrong.* Harmondsworth, Middlesex, England: Penguin Books.

Martin, Rex. 1985. *Rawls and Rights.* Lawrence, Kans.: University of Kansas Press.

Maynard Smith, John, & G. R. Price, 1973. "The Logic of Animal Conflicts." *Nature* 246:15–18.

——— 1976. "Evolution and the Theory of Games." *American Scientist* 64: 41–45.

Milinski, Manfred. 1993. "Cooperation wins and stays." *Nature* 364: 12–13.

Milton, Katharine. 1993. "Diet and Primate Evolution." *Scientific American,* August 1993, 86–92.

Morris, Herbert. 1968. "Persons and Punishment." *The Monist* 52 (October 1968): 475–501. Reprinted in Joel Feinberg and Hyman Gross, ed. *Philosophy of Law.* Belmont, Calif.: Wadsworth Publishing Co., 1975.

Narveson, Jan. 1988. *The Libertarian Idea.* Philadelphia: Temple University Press.

Nowak, Martin, & Karl Sigmund. 1993. "A strategy of win-stay, lose-shift that outperforms tit-for-tat in the Prisoner's Dilemma game." *Nature* 364: 56–58.

Nozick, Robert. 1974. *Anarchy, State, and Utopia.* New York: Basic Books.

Poundstone, William. 1992. *Prisoner's Dilemma.* New York: Doubleday.

Rawls, John. 1971. *A Theory of Justice.* Cambridge: Harvard University Press.

——— 1993. *Political Liberalism.* New York: Columbia University Press.

Rescher, Nicholas. 1980. "The Canons of Distributive Justice." In *Justice: Alternative Political Perspectives,* ed. James P. Sterba, 33–40. Belmont, Calif.: Wadsworth Publishing Co.

Scarr, Sandra, and Richard A. Weinberg. 1978. "Attitudes, Interests, and I.Q." *Human Nature,* April 1978.

Trivers, Robert. 1971. "The Evolution of Reciprocal Altruism." *Quarterly Review of Biology* 46: 35–57.

——— 1985. *Social Evolution.* Menlo Park, Calif.: Benjamin/Cummings.

Wilson, Edward O. 1975. *Sociobiology: The New Synthesis.* Cambridge: Harvard University Press.

——— 1978. *On Human Nature.* Cambridge: Harvard University Press.

Wilson, James Q. 1993. *The Moral Sense.* New York: Free Press.

Index

About the Author

Howard Kahane (A.B. and M.A., UCLA; PhD., University of Pennsylvania) is a retired professor of Philosophy, having taught at the City University of New York, the University of Kansas, Whitman College, and the University of Maryland at Baltimore County. He is the author of several very widely adopted philosophy textbooks, including *Logic and Contemporary Rhetoric: The Use of Reason in Everyday Life* and *Logic and Philosophy: A Modern Introduction* (both now in their seventh editions), and of many journal articles and other philosophical essays, including "Making the World Safe for Reciprocity" and "Sociobiology, Egoism and Reciprocity".